W9-CYT-955

Problem-Based
Learning
in K-8 Classrooms

A Teacher's Guide to Implementation

HOW

why

Where

What

Ann Lambros

Problem-Based
Learning
in K-8 Classrooms

**CORWIN
PRESS**

The Corwin Press logo—a raven striding across an open book—represents the happy union of courage and learning. We are a professional-level publisher of books and journals for K-12 educators, and we are committed to creating and providing resources that embody these qualities. Corwin's motto is "Success for All Learners."

Problem-Based
Learning
in K-8 Classrooms

A Teacher's Guide to Implementation

Ann Lambros

CORWIN PRESS, INC.
A Sage Publications Company
Thousand Oaks, California

For information:

Corwin Press, Inc.
A Sage Publications Company
2455 Teller Road
Thousand Oaks, California 91320
E-mail: order@corwinpress.com

Sage Publications Ltd.
6 Bonhill Street
London EC2A 4PU
United Kingdom

Sage Publications India Pvt. Ltd.
M-32 Market
Greater Kailash I
New Delhi 110 048 India

Printed in the United States of America

Library of Congress Cataloging-in-Publication Data

Lambros, Ann.
    Problem-based learning in K-8 classrooms: A teacher's guide to implementation / Ann Lambros.
        p. cm.
    Includes bibliographical references and index.
    ISBN 0-7619-4533-4 (c) — ISBN 0-7619-4534-2 (p)
    1. Problem-based learning. 2. Problem-solving—Study and teaching (Elementary)   I. Title.
    LB1027.42 .L36 2002
    372.13—dc21
                                2001005177

This book is printed on acid-free paper.

01   02   03   04   05   06   07   7   6   5   4   3   2   1

Editor-at-Large:	Mark Goldberg
Corwin Editor:	Faye Zucker
Editorial Assistant:	Julia Parnell
Production Editor:	Olivia Weber
Typesetter/Designer:	Denyse Dunn
Indexer:	Pamela Van Huss
Cover Designer:	Michael Dubowe
Copy Editor:	Rachel Hile Bassett

● Contents ■

● Preface ■

Observe almost any elementary or middle school at the end of the school day and what you are likely to see is children exiting with seemingly endless energy from the schoolhouse doors. Behind those same doors are nearly exhausted teachers who are spent from providing direct instruction to children throughout much of the school day. Too often, and in many traditional teaching styles, the teacher is doing a disproportionate amount of the work. The learners are often passive, waiting for direction or waiting for the opportunity to respond to the teacher.

One common outcome is that children do not know what to do when confronted with any type of uncertainty. At the first moment of doubt, the student's hand flies into the air. Teachers then spend an inordinate amount of time and energy going from student to student to assist each in moving forward with the task at hand. This scene repeats itself far too often throughout the day, explaining why teachers become so weary by day's end while their students are still bursting with energy.

Problem-based learning (PBL) is a teaching and learning style that addresses the deficient elements of this scenario. In the PBL approach, students are presented with a loosely structured problem and work in small groups to arrive at some resolution to the problem. The teacher is no longer the focus of all that happens, although the teacher plays a crucial role in selecting the problem and facilitating the student groups. Rather, the students determine the kind of content learning required to move forward, the resources to use, and how new information is synthesized toward resolution. As a result, the students participate actively in their own learning, create their own direction as driven by the problem scenario, and continuously respond and react to each other as well as to the teacher and to the new content information they encounter.

Far from being a new technique, many of the characteristics and principles of PBL were described as early as 1916 by John Dewey. He was convinced that such an approach would create the highest level of learning among all children by tapping their interests, previous knowledge, and connection to their own world of meaning. One element of PBL is that the problem scenario exists within the real world of the learner, effectively eliminating the students' often-posed question, "Why do we need to know this?"

PBL enlarges the scope of learning opportunities for students at all levels of education. Though PBL originated in medical schools, there are various organized movements nationwide to integrate the methodology in K-12 classrooms. PBL is becoming well established as a valuable addition to traditional teaching methods and has moved beyond the "flavor-of-the-month" trend so often seen in educational reform attempts.

One example of a plan to use PBL in education reform is in the mission of the Center of Excellence for Research, Teaching, and Learning (CERTL) at Wake Forest University School of Medicine in Winston-Salem, North Carolina. Its mission includes providing intensive and continuous professional development for K-12 educators in PBL and sponsoring enrichment programs anchored in PBL activities for K-12 students. CERTL has also sponsored the development of PBL instructional materials by teachers for teachers and manages the dissemination of those materials for classroom use. Examples of these classroom materials are found throughout this book.

Another example of educators' extensive interest in PBL is reflected in the participation of more than 600 college and public school faculty at an international PBL 2000 conference hosted by Samford University in Birmingham, Alabama. Nine countries and 30 states were represented. Without question, at least several thousand schools and colleges are interested in including PBL in their teaching repertoires. In the past 10 years, several hundred U.S. schools have included PBL in their repertoire, and several books on PBL in K-12 education and teacher training have been published (see References and Suggested Readings).

The American Association for Higher Education established an organization in 1990 called the Education Trust as a special project to encourage colleges and universities to support K-12 reform. One of their most recognized slogans, "College Begins in Kindergarten," advances the responsibility of educators to provide continuity of educational experiences that best prepare the student for the next level. It is not too great a leap to see the benefit of implementing a pedagogy such as PBL, which can serve learners from kindergarten through college and beyond.

This book is designed to familiarize educators with the philosophy of PBL, to show its intended benefits, and to present many classroom examples. The focus is on the use of PBL in K-8 classrooms. Examples of PBL problem scenarios and the ways they are used by experienced PBL teachers are provided. The experiences of these PBL teachers will demonstrate the variety of possibilities for integrating PBL into current teaching strategies.

Acknowledgments

A remarkable number of individuals have contributed to the writing of this book. I would like to thank each of them for sharing so generously of their time, energy, and experiences. I would also like to thank them for their commitment to improving the quality of education for all learners.

I am especially grateful to Dr. Stan Hill. It was his vision and determination that created the many opportunities for teacher growth, student enrichment, and my own professional and personal development around this project.

I also express the deepest appreciation to the many, many teachers who committed hours of their time and creative energy to authoring PBL problems over the past 5 years. It never ceases to amaze me that these folks can spend a full day teaching and nurturing children and then work another 4 hours, with seemingly endless energy, to create instructional materials in hopes of making things better for students. I am indebted to Brenda Crumpler for her tireless support. Her willingness to read, reread, and read again each chapter as it was drafted goes far beyond the expectations of friendship.

My thanks also go to Townley Sledge and Margaret Connor for all their assistance in locating and delivering materials at every request I made. Their commitment as pioneers in uncharted PBL territory should also be acknowledged. Nearly 7 years ago, they were members of the first teacher team to author PBL cases for this project, and they have remained steadfast in their efforts ever since.

Last but not least, I wish to thank Mark Goldberg, editor-at-large for Corwin Press, for his patient guidance and always helpful feedback throughout the process of writing this book.

● About the Author ■

Ann Lambros, PhD, is currently the Director of the Center of Excellence for Research, Teaching, and Learning at the Wake Forest University School of Medicine, where she is also a faculty member. Her extensive experience with problem-based learning (PBL) began in 1987 when the medical school adopted a PBL curriculum for medical students. Since then, Dr. Lambros has conducted more than 150 professional development seminars in PBL for faculty in professional schools, 4-year universities, community colleges, and K-12 institutions. She now spends much of her time as a consultant in developing PBL curricula at every level of formal education, from kindergarten through professional and graduate school.

Dr. Lambros can be reached at the Center of Excellence for Research, Teaching, and Learning (CERTL Office) at the Wake Forest University School of Medicine, Medical Center Boulevard, Winston-Salem, NC 27157, USA; telephone: 336-716-3993; e-mail: alambros@wfubmc.edu.

To my daughter, Adrienne—
She is the reason I was born.

and

To Stewart,
Whose steadfast love and support
are my most precious gifts.

●◆ 1 ▲■

The What and Why of Problem-Based Learning

The Teacher's part, then, in the process of instruction is that of a guide, director or superintendent of the operations by which the pupil teaches himself.

—Joseph Payne, 1883,
Lectures on the Science and Art of Education

A Defining Moment

A practical place to begin the conversation about what problem-based learning (PBL) is and why it enhances traditional teaching approaches is with a working definition.

PBL is a method based on the principle of using problems as the starting point for the acquisition of new knowledge. Pivotal to its effectiveness is the use of problems that create learning through both new experience and the reinforcement of existing knowledge. Situations that are in the learner's real world are presented as problems and stimulate the need to seek out new information and synthesize it in the context of the problem scenario.

A simple example might be the situation in which you require driving directions to somewhere you have never been. You begin the process with what you already know or your existing knowledge: where you will start driving and where you intend to arrive. You then identify what you need to know to effectively and efficiently reach your destination: names of streets and highways, distinguishing landmarks to look for, and perhaps the mileage you should anticipate. You then integrate this information with your existing knowledge, for example, the amount of time it typically takes you to travel the number of miles given the type of road conditions you can expect. Often, after creating the experience of using the new information to travel a new route and successfully arrive at the appointed destination, you can then retrieve this new information and apply it to similar situations. It is also likely that you will retain much of the new information and be able to successfully travel the same route again when the need arises.

The real-world frame of reference for you in the example above is that it is likely you have had to acquire and follow driving directions unfamiliar to you before. Each learner has his or her own real-world frame of reference that should be attended to when PBL problem scenarios are developed and used in the classroom. The frame of reference of a 6-year-old is obviously quite different from that of an 11-year-old, but it is just as significant for the effective use of PBL.

There are further characteristics that define and determine the quality of how PBL shows up in classroom instruction. It is essential that the learners determine their own learning needs, or learning issues, based on the problem they encounter. This is the student-centered element of PBL. In the earlier driving example, imagine that someone else determined the directions you needed without taking into account your own existing knowledge. The information that person decided to provide you could discount your starting point, your familiarity with some of the route, or your own travel preferences. In essence, the person would be telling you what he or she thinks you need to know, with little regard for what you think you need to know. To get excellent information, you must get answers to the questions that will help you. If this sounds familiar, it is because as educators we spend quite a lot of time telling our learners what they need to know without first determining what they already know or what they think they need to know.

Teachers are often nervous about this notion of allowing students to determine what they need to know or which learning areas they will pursue. They ask, "How do you know that students will come up with appropriate learning issues, or how can a teacher be certain that the intended content areas will be included?" PBL problem scenarios do not stand alone but are designed and facilitated by the teacher. Effective facilitation will prompt students into the intended learning areas, if necessary. Examples of effective PBL problem scenarios and instructional units are provided by grade level in the following chapters. The qualities and characteristics of effective PBL problem scenarios and their development are described in a later chapter as well.

The PBL approach also requires that students work in small groups to attain their learning objectives. Teachers will be further reassured about how learning issues are identified when they observe that within groups, the learning needs tend to be somewhat diversified. The learning needs of one student complement those of another as the group works together to address all of the learning issues.

As these small groups become the focus of the learning situation in classrooms, teachers must assume a different and sometimes unfamiliar role. Rather than being the sole content authority directing the learning process, the teacher now becomes the facilitator or coach of each small group. Suggestions for effective facilitation skills will be offered throughout the book.

Collaboration within the group is an element of PBL that is necessary to accomplish problem resolution. This is a lifelong skill that makes sense to begin developing and practicing as early as kindergarten. The type of intended collaboration in the small group includes resource identification, peer support, acknowledgment and continued reinforcement of existing knowledge, and assistance and assurance in integrating and synthesizing new information. The formation of small groups, their dynamics, and how well they function are all important considerations in the

PBL process. Because these elements are dependent on the learners' developmental stage, the principles to consider will be presented chapter by chapter as they relate to grade level.

The last essential element of PBL is that in the process, students must take responsibility and be held accountable for their own learning. Once the students have identified their own learning issues, it is fundamental to the success of PBL to make them accountable for that learning in meaningful ways. Students must be able to demonstrate that within the process they have acquired new content and that they can apply that new information toward problem resolution. Creating the situations that allow students to acquire new content and demonstrate application constitutes an entire chapter dedicated to authentic assessment strategies.

The Why Behind PBL

There are philosophical underpinnings to the PBL process that explain why one would choose to make a shift to PBL in the classroom. In *How to Use Problem-Based Learning in the Classroom,* Delisle (1997) gives a thorough and informative description of the how and why of PBL in the classroom. In this book, the focus will be a more practical overview of why shifting to PBL practices in the classroom creates advantages for both the learners and the teacher.

PBL creates opportunities in the classroom that traditional approaches simply do not. The most significant is the relevance of the learning that occurs. Because the problem scenarios are from the real world and because the students determine their own learning needs, the learning that occurs is highly relevant. This contributes to holding the students' interest, developing a deeper understanding of the content, and increasing the retention of new information.

The emphasis in PBL is on conceptual understanding rather than the memorization of facts. The intended learning is presented through the problem scenario in a way that leads the student to want to know and need to know the new information, much like the driver who needs directions. The problem then requires the students to use the new information to present resolutions to the problem. As the students work in their small groups toward solutions, they must collaborate and negotiate within the group to rule in and rule out viable solutions. They learn to create functional relationships with each other to accomplish the group's goals. Students develop communication skills and more sophisticated interpersonal skills. They develop respect for one another's contributions and find ways to acknowledge and encourage each other.

In addition to these benefits, students report that they become excited about resolving the math or science or political problems and about discovering new information that helps in figuring out what is going on in the problem. Discovery, fun, and excitement are all elements that most learners prefer to have as part of instruction. We tend to work harder and longer on the endeavors that we enjoy. When students work longer and harder, they learn more and are more likely to be able to use the new information in similar contexts and situations. Also, teachers are assured that students have learned when they can apply new content.

Another outcome for students is the development of a process for lifelong learning. Students become aware that they are able to figure out what they need to know, to find what they need to know, and to use this new information to create solutions in situations that have no obvious answer. They grow more confident in their abilities in these areas and soon are engaging the process even outside the classroom.

A parent shared the story of how her third grader helped to figure out the type of gift to buy a coworker by asking PBL questions: What does she like? What does she not like? Where do you find the kinds of things she likes? What is her favorite color? How much money can you spend? Does she have kids, pets, and so on? This young student was using the process of determining what was known, what additional information was needed, and what resources were available. The significance of this example is that the student was concerned not about getting the answer right but rather about collecting information to pose questions that would lead to "right" answers.

This leads us to the most significant benefit of using PBL. Focusing on multiple solutions rather than on correct answers allows students to be successful in ways that have not been available to them in traditional approaches. There are limited opportunities to be considered successful in most classrooms. Success tends to be defined by the highest scores, the most right answers, the neatest work, and, often, the most conventional work. Although there is value in high scores, correct answers, and neatness, there is also value in creativity, discovery, contribution to a process, and contribution to the development of other people. Students not only are afforded these opportunities in the PBL process but are positively acknowledged as they engage the opportunities. We all have the tendency to return to and continue the things that make us feel successful. Students return to PBL each time feeling more confident, motivated, and excited about what they are able to accomplish.

The PBL Process in Action

When observing a PBL lesson, it is sometimes difficult for the novice to discern the underlying structure. There are actually very specific components to the process that are there to ensure that the principles underlying PBL remain intact.

A typical PBL session will begin in this fashion: The students, either as a large group or in small groups of five to seven students each, encounter the PBL problem scenario. The delivery of the scenario may vary from projecting the problem using an overhead projector, to a PowerPoint projection, to providing a hard copy of the problem scenario to each student or student group. For a fourth-grade class, the problem might be as modest as this:

> The PTA has given your class $50 to run a class store selling school supplies. Your group must plan a presentation with visual aids about how the store should be run, what will be sold in the store, and how the profits should be used. You should start with an inventory of ten items to sell. Following the presentations, the class will vote on how to best operate the store and spend the profits.

One student reads the problem aloud. This accomplishes several things: One student practices reading aloud, and the other students and the teacher follow along so there is confidence that all have heard and read the same problem without omitting key words or skipping sentences. PBL is a student-centered method, so it is always a student who reads the problem.

Once the students have encountered the problem, they proceed to create at least two lists. One is headed "Facts" and should itemize all of the facts they have been given in the problem. This helps them begin to identify what they know. They then make a list headed "Need to Know," in which they list all the information they would like to have to better understand the problem and their role in resolving the problem. From this "Need to Know" list, students should begin to derive a "Learning Issues" list of the things they need to look up, research, or explore in order to move forward with problem resolution. Following the exploration phase, the students should then list their "Possible Solutions." This list will have ideas about how to resolve the problem and should require the development of a new "Learning Issues" list. This new list is used to gather additional information that will allow the students to rule in or rule out the possible solutions they created (see Table 1.1).

Here is an example of a seventh-grade science problem regarding weather and the process for working through it.

You are a weather forecaster in Morehead, North Carolina. You are currently concerned about a tropical storm off the coast of Africa. You must track and predict where it is going and when it will strike land. Once you have collected this information, you must give warnings to ships and military aircraft that could be affected by the storm.

The students' Facts list may contain things such as: We are weather forecasters; we are in Morehead, North Carolina; there is a tropical storm; and the storm is near Africa. The Need to Know list may contain questions such as: Where is Morehead, North Carolina? Where is the storm on Africa's coast? How fast is the storm moving? There are additional facts that may be supplied to the students by providing them with maps and other information. The Learning Issues list may contain things such as: What makes a storm tropical? How are storms classified? What affects storms' movements? From these learning issues, the

Table 1.1 PBL Process

Facts List	Need to Know	Learning Issues

Possible Solutions	New Learning Issues

Defendable Solution(s)

This or a similar form is the basic document in the PBL process. It may be structured slightly differently or it may take two to three pages, but the categories are constant. See Appendix C for an example of a filled-in chart.

students might gather information about barometric pressures, ocean currents, and wind scale. They will further explore geographic issues around the landfall of the storm and where the potentially affected military bases are located. They will use mathematical equations to determine storm speed as they predict its movements. After gathering this kind of new information, students will make their list of possible solutions. In this case, that list might contain two or three hypotheses about where the storm will land. Then, in the context of the problem scenario, students should be provided with enough additional information about the storm's movements to eventually choose one of their hypotheses as the most viable.

Throughout this process, the teacher's role is very active as the facilitator and guide. Sometimes the teacher may take the role of "expert resource" in order to provide some of the needed information. For the most part, however, the teacher is monitoring the process and progress of the students, helping them to explore the intended learning objectives, and reassuring them or redirecting them as needed. It is important to understand that the teacher is anything but absent from the dynamics and effectiveness of this learning approach. The teacher is pivotal to the opportunities available to the students in the PBL methodology.

In a Nutshell

The intent in this book is to provide teachers with an understanding of the PBL process and with sample instructional materials to support classroom implementation. Chapters 2 through 5 will address these issues by grade level, giving special attention to the developmental characteristics of young learners. The additional elements that contribute to the success of PBL instruction, such as group size, group work, supporting content learning, timing, pacing, and the teacher's role, will be discussed by grade level as well.

Chapter 6 will provide an overview of the appropriate and effective use of authentic assessment techniques and PBL. Sample evaluation tools and strategies are provided as well as assessment templates specific to evaluating the student's process skills and group function levels. Guidance for evaluating students as individuals and for evaluating a student's group performance are discussed. Also included in this chapter is information about assessing the effectiveness of PBL as an instructional approach. Many teachers are concerned about being able to determine if the methodology is working in their classroom. How does a teacher know if a student is learning more, retaining more, and becoming able to apply more and be a better collaborator or negotiator as a result of engaging the PBL methodology? This chapter also makes the point that there can be very strong linkage between local and state standards and PBL. PBL is a powerful method that can work with almost any curriculum.

●◆2▲■

PBL and the K-1 Classroom

It is important that students bring a certain ragamuffin, barefoot, irreverence to their studies; they are not here to worship what is known, but to question it.

—Jacob Bronowski, 1973,
The Ascent of Man

Getting Started in the K-1 Classroom

Two keys to the effective use of PBL are problem selection and facilitation. The successful execution of either or both of these is in knowing the characteristics of your learners. Problems should be selected that appeal to the developmental level of your students.

In the K-1 classroom, effective problems are often embedded in stories or are storybook based. Children at these ages love stories, and they enjoy repetition. They also enjoy fantasy and the opportunity to pretend. The role of the student in PBL problems at this level will often have them pretend to be someone other than themselves. This is demonstrated in several of the examples provided.

Another feature of PBL problems for these young learners is the opportunity for the student to discover something as the problem scenario unfolds. Because these children have limited skills for researching the learning issues they identify, subsequent parts of the scenario may reveal information in a format that has the student "discover" new content. An example of this is provided in the problem below titled *Who Stole the Cookies From the Cookie Jar?*

Young students often have rather modest attention spans. Most PBL problems accommodate this characteristic by having the children engage in an activity that is related to the problem. Children may listen to a story, watch a video, draw a picture, or sing a song. The examples in this chapter include descriptions of some related activities, but the teacher should feel free to replace or supplement suggested activities with his or her own favorites that are problem relevant. Teachers know their own students very well; know what works well with their students; and have favorite strategies, lessons, and projects for their students.

Introducing the problem to K-1 students is usually best done with either an overhead projector or a flipchart-sized poster. The teacher often reads the problem to the class or has the class read along with her (depending on reading levels of the students). If a classroom assistant is available, it is best to split the class in half as students proceed to make the lists of Facts, Need to Know, and Ideas/Solutions. During the development of these lists, the teacher should prod the students to consider things that will lead them to the intended content or objectives of the problem. Once these lists are completed, the introduction of a resource or activity usually moves the students along to the discovery phase of the problem.

Students are helped during the list-making phase to identify the facts that are supplied in the problem, to formulate as many questions as possible to address the Need to Know areas, and to generate ideas or solutions that might resolve the problem. The critical thinking process is facilitated by having children revise the Need to Know (or Learning Issues) list throughout the problem. As new information is acquired, some learning issues are resolved, whereas others are generated. The teacher should encourage the students to develop learning issues that will help them to rule in or rule out any of the potential solutions.

Initially, helping students to work with a small group and to be problem solvers feels slightly unnatural to many teachers. Remember, we are mostly accustomed to telling students what they need to know and when they need to know it and addressing them individually rather than as a group. Facilitation skills will develop and feel more natural the more often PBL is used in the classroom. Appendix A contains suggested "Facilitator Do" and "Facilitator Don't" behaviors that might be a useful reference while getting started.

It Looks Like This

Here is an example of a PBL problem used in a kindergarten classroom. It could just as easily be used in the first grade or in a combination class. The teacher who presented this problem had never introduced PBL in her classroom before this lesson.

The teacher reads the PBL scenario aloud to the class from a flipchart page.

You are the foreman of the Oink!Oink! construction company. You have been asked to build a wolfproof house.

What materials and shapes will you use?
You will need to draw the house you plan to build.

The intended objectives of this problem are for the children to explore a variety of shapes and materials and to determine the properties of materials. The teacher chose not to use small groups for this problem and instead left the class in a large group of 18. The children left their desks and sat in a semicircle at the front of the room as the teacher introduced the problem.

After reading the problem aloud and together, the children were asked if they understood what a foreman was. They did not and were told by the teacher that the foreman is the boss of the construction team.

Notice that two critical elements of problem development and selection are apparent in this PBL scenario. First, in the world of five- and six-year-olds, it is important to have a wolf-proof house because they are familiar with the story "The Three Little Pigs." If children are not familiar with the story, simply read the story to them before introducing this problem. Second, the children have been given the role of "boss." Five- and six-year-olds are rarely the boss of anything, and they are delighted to have the opportunity to pretend to be the boss in this problem.

The teacher then asked the class to tell her the things that should go on the list called "Facts." She had already lettered chart paper and taped it to the board. The children supplied her with the few facts from this problem: They were the foreman, they had to build a wolfproof house, and they had to draw the house.

Next, she helped them to create the Need to Know/Learning Issues list by asking them what would be helpful to know to design such a house. The children listed things such as: What are houses usually made of? Can wolves blow down most houses? Where do wolves live? What shapes can houses be?

Then the teacher asked the students for ideas about the shapes and materials they would use to go on the Ideas/Solutions list. The children suggested square, round, and triangular houses. One child suggested a diamond-shaped house. When the teacher asked how that would work, the child offered that the bottom half of the diamond would be underground and so would prevent the house from tipping over if the wolf blew on it. This is a good example of higher-order thinking, which typically is not demonstrated in K-1 classrooms, primarily for lack of opportunity.

The children were then asked about the kinds of materials they would use. They suggested bricks (which worked in the original story), steel, really hard wood (to distinguish it from the sticks used in the original story), and ice. Ice was explained as a good material because the wolf would slide off the house before he could get into it through the chimney (which happens with the brick house in the original story).

During this conversation, one of the children said, "It really doesn't matter what you make the house of, the wolf will just go in the door." Another child responded, "Wolves can't open doors!" The first child declared, "They do it all the time on TV." The teacher asked the first child where she had seen this on TV, and it turned out to be in cartoons. The teacher captured this chance to address some unintended learning issues by asking the children the differences between wolves in cartoons and wolves that live in the wild. It was clear that there was some confusion over the distinguishing characteristics, and so the teacher asked the students where they might find this information.

The children had ideas to read a book, watch a video, watch the Discovery Channel, ask a veterinarian, and to ask "that person that will come to your neighborhood and take away an animal that doesn't belong there" or a wild animal control specialist. They were so eager to know the true differences between cartoon wolves and real wolves that they asked the teacher if she would find a book to read them after lunch. This is a great example of student-centered learning, in which the children have readily identified learning areas that they want to have resolved. Even though this part of the lesson was unintended, the teacher considered it valuable enough and well enough aligned with other objectives to get several books from the library for the afternoon reading time.

The children were then directed back to their desk clusters, where they were to draw a picture of their wolfproof house. They were told that when the drawings were complete, each student would show his or her drawing to the class and explain why the design was wolfproof. The children spent approximately 15 minutes on this activity and in discussing at their desks as they drew the various wolfproof features of their designs.

A delightful example of further problem solving occurred with one child, who preferred to follow the teacher about the room or watch his classmates rather than draw his own picture. The teacher suggested that he needed to draw his picture instead of wandering around, but he said he was still deciding. A few minutes later she encouraged him again to start his picture. (He was not being disruptive but merely observing what was going on around him and what his classmates were drawing.) Soon the teacher warned the little guy that it was about time to show pictures to the class, and he would have nothing to show if he did not hurry and complete a picture. His response was, "That's OK, really. My house is invisible, and that's why it's wolfproof."

This example demonstrates the process for introducing a PBL problem in the K-1 classroom and provides some ideas about what to anticipate from the students. It also illustrates that the problems are designed with very intentional content objectives and that often, quite significant unintentional content objectives present themselves. Further, it shows the ways in which PBL makes available chances for students to demonstrate what they already know and how they are already thinking critically.

More Examples

One PBL-experienced kindergarten teacher recently shared that she often turns her students' questions about one thing or another into a PBL problem. She then lets that problem drive the learning to answer the presented questions. This teacher is quite the exception, creating PBL problems "on her feet." Most teachers prefer to look over prepared problems, anticipate the resources the students may need, set up related activities, and have a clear sense of the directions in which they will facilitate the problem.

There are two primary sources for prepared problems. One source is the problems developed by other PBL teachers. Many schools keep a file of these. Another source is to prepare one's own problems. Chapter 7 addresses the specifics of authoring your own problems. In the meantime, here are two more examples of PBL problem scenarios that have been used successfully in K-1 classrooms. Of course, for each example (and for others in the book), teachers will use the outline given in Table 1.1 (PBL Process), emphasizing those areas the teacher feels are most important for a particular lesson.

Who Stole the Cookies From the Cookie Jar? addresses the following objectives: likenesses and differences among individuals, describing likenesses and differences, sorting by given attributes, using language for critical analysis and evaluation, and integrity as a personal characteristic or value. The scenario for this problem is as follows:

> Cookies have disappeared from the classroom cookie jar. You have been called in to investigate the case. There were several eyewitnesses to the crime. Each person has a different description of the thief. Everyone in the room is a possible suspect. Your job is to question the eyewitnesses, eliminate the suspects, and identify the culprit.

This problem scenario contains the following eyewitness statements as resources for the students.

> Eyewitness 1: I saw someone go into the room. The suspect was less than 5 feet tall. It had two arms and two legs. It was wearing bright colors. It had one head with two eyes and two ears.
>
> Eyewitness 2: I saw the same things, but I am sure the suspect was less than 4 feet tall. Its ears were rounded. It had dark eyes.
>
> Eyewitness 3: Yes, I saw all that, but I'm sure the suspect was less than 3 feet tall. It had very short hair. Its ears were more to the top of its head. Its hair was more than one color.
>
> Eyewitness 4: I agree with all of that. The suspect was about 2 feet tall. It was carrying some kind of backpack. It was wearing a red jacket or sweater. It must have been in a fight or something because I noticed two black eyes.

The culprit in this problem turns out to be one of the stuffed animals or characters in the classroom. The eyewitnesses are also dolls or stuffed animals, and their accounts are modified to match whatever the teacher has chosen to be the thief. Children eliminate each other as suspects when they realize the height is too short to be a classmate.

Measuring to distinguish between the different reported heights is usually an activity associated with this problem.

Sorting games or activities are usually provided. There may be a story read about how people are different.

Once the students have identified the culprit, there is usually a conversation about why it is wrong to take things that do not belong to us and what are appropriate consequences for doing so. The problem usually concludes with rewarding the children for solving the crime with the cookies that have been recovered.

Weather Watch is a good example of a PBL problem that might be used to introduce a weather unit and/or a safety unit. Here is the problem scenario:

> You are at home one evening with a teenaged baby-sitter watching TV. A warning message comes across the TV screen. It says that the National Weather Service has issued a Severe Thunderstorm/Tornado Watch with the possibility of flooding in your county.
>
> > What will you do to prepare for the storm?
> > How does a thunderstorm or tornado cause flooding?
> > What other types of weather can cause flooding?
> > What other types of weather can be harmful?
> > Devise a safe plan for this possible storm.

In preparing their lists, the children are likely to include a variety of weather patterns. They typically have limited knowledge of the specifics of these phenomena. There are several children's books that are good resources to address these learning issues. They include *Flash, Crash, Rumble, and Roll; Tornado Alert; Weather Words; The Big Storm; Hurricanes;* and *Twisters.* Appendix E has complete bibliographical information for these and other PBL resources.

After collecting the additional information about dangerous weather, the children are helped to make a safe plan for what to do during severe weather situations. This is a good group activity. Three or four students work together to pool their ideas or knowledge about safety and what a good safety plan might be. Children will need help in capturing or documenting their ideas for a safe plan. They might make drawings or create an audio recording of their plan. Each group presents their plan to the entire class and explains the specific safety features.

The possibilities for learning objectives in PBL problems such as this one are wide, and they are determined primarily by how the problem is facilitated. If the emphasis is on safety, there may be less time spent on the discussion of severe weather. If the emphasis is on weather, devising a safety plan may be a wrap-up activity to a week's worth of study of various weather patterns and how they might become dangerous.

Types of PBL Problems

Most PBL problems afford the teacher these kinds of choices. Once the teacher has become comfortable with using PBL and facilitating rather than directing, the learning possibilities within many problems are typically extensive, although other problems may be quite focused and have very specific learning objectives. Broad problems with many potential learning issues are initially more difficult to facilitate and are typically more challenging to the students. Focused problems often require less direct facilitation, and the children have a clearer sense of the directions they will choose for learning.

An example of each type of problem is given here to illustrate the differences.

Problem 1. Where's the Great Pumpkin? (An Open-Ended Problem)

The scenario is:

Your class has been getting pumpkins to decorate and carve each fall from a farmer at Baa Moo Farm. This year, however, he has no pumpkins at all to sell. He explains to your teacher that the pumpkin crop rotted before they were ready to harvest this year. He wonders if your class can help him figure out what happened.

Students prepare their lists and hear the story "Bring in the Pumpkins." They learn that the farmer keeps animals and that animals often attract insects. If the children have additional questions for the farmer, they prepare a list, and the teacher promises to find out the answers that evening. On the second day, the students hear the story "Lots of Rot." They may then add to their list of possible ideas or solutions. Each child then works with a partner to think of ways to solve the farmer's problem, and the pairs present their ideas to the class. The class, working as a large group, then prepares a letter to send to the farmer with all of the information they have learned and their best solutions.

The learning issues for this problem may include science-related objectives concerning plant life, living and nonliving organisms, and environmental issues. Potential math-related objectives include estimation, measurements of the patch, number of seeds planted within the area of the patch, and making predictions. Concepts of collecting data, analyzing information, and evaluation are included as potential learning areas, as are communication skills for sharing their problem-solving ideas. Teachers are likely to see many more possibilities in this particular problem.

Problem 2. The Terrible Toothache
(A More Focused Problem)

This problem is popular in the month of February, National Dental Health Month. In this problem, the teacher asks the children to help her help a friend. She tells them:

> I was eating with a friend of mine last night. We were having an apple for dessert. All of a sudden, she said, "Ouch! I can't eat this apple. My tooth really hurts when I bite into it. That's never happened before. I wonder why it hurts like this now?" I told her that we have been talking about teeth and how to take care of them and that I would ask you why her tooth might be hurting.

First the children list the facts they know and then the things they would like to know. Most of their Need to Know items are initially about how the friend takes care of her teeth, the kinds of things she likes to eat, and if she goes to the dentist. The teacher should be prepared to supply this information to the students. The teacher may then help the children to add items to the list about what makes a tooth hurt. Do they know what decay is? Where does decay come from? How do you prevent decay? Are there other things that might make your mouth sore?

Different resources are appropriate for addressing these questions. Often during February, a public health dental hygienist schedules a classroom visit. This problem might be timed to coincide with such a visit, and the hygienist becomes an excellent resource for these questions. There are also videotapes and books on dental health and proper tooth care that might be used.

After the children have learned about tooth decay and the other related issues, they use two white paper bags to draw an unhealthy mouth and a healthy mouth. The bags are inverted so they fit on the students' hands puppet style. The children share with the class their drawings and explain why one mouth is unhealthy and the other is healthy. The teacher may then choose some sample bags to share with her friend to illustrate what may happen if she neglects her teeth or what may happen if she takes care of them.

This problem is quite focused and can be done in a morning or afternoon. Problems that are more open ended, with a broader list of potential learning areas, are often extended over 2 or 3 days. Problems should not be extended for too long, however, as students will begin to lose interest in the original problem scenario and become task driven rather than self-directed in their learning.

Problem 3. We'll Take Care of It
(An Extended Problem)

An additional problem design is the ongoing problem that requires regular revisiting. In this example, the children are given this scenario:

We may be able to get a pet for our classroom. The health department regulations will not let us have a pet that is not in a self-contained habitat. We will need to feed and care for our pet. It will have to stay at school (even when we are not here). We need to agree on the best pet for our room.

The teachers who choose this problem are usually prepared to actually acquire the agreed-upon pet. This not only makes the problem a real one but gives the children the opportunity to care for the pet and carry out the plans they make about being responsible pet owners.

The intended objectives include learning how to care for living organisms, participating in decision making, understanding responsibility, organizing and applying information, and considering health risks that some animals may present. An accompanying story, "Franklin Wants a Pet," gives the children some ideas about the kinds of things they will need to know and consider in choosing a pet. The teacher facilitates the children from their Need to Know list to include viable suggestions on their Ideas/Solutions list. Children often agree on a gerbil, hamster, or fish. They then organize a care plan before the pet is acquired. This plan is used as a guide for caring for the pet. The children have a lot of ownership with the plan because they devised it themselves. If concerns eventually arise about the care and maintenance of the pet, the teacher can have the children revisit, and perhaps even revise, their original plan. This way, the children remain accountable for their decision and their plan.

Problem 4. Crunch, Munch, a Healthy Lunch (A Culminating Problem)

The last example is a favorite of PBL teachers and students because of its culminating activity—a classroom picnic. Following an instructional unit on nutrition, the children are given this problem:

> What can we do as a class to celebrate the good work we have done and show what we have learned?

The students have already learned something about using the food pyramid, identifying foods by using the senses, and identifying health-promoting foods. The teacher facilitates the children into showing what they have learned by planning a menu for a class picnic. The children plan to prepare as much of the menu as possible in the classroom and the remainder at home.

They choose a day and come with blankets, paper products, and their assigned foods for the classroom picnic.

This is a good example of wrapping up a unit of instruction by using a PBL problem. Doing so allows the children to connect what they have been learning to a real-world event of their own. The students also have an opportunity to demonstrate what they learned and how they are able to apply the new content. Other basic objectives are included, such as planning, organizing, following a recipe, measuring for recipes, and making good choices in food decisions.

Remember that a PBL problem can be used effectively at any time within an area of instruction. The teacher may open a unit with a PBL problem, wrap up a unit with a PBL problem, or choose to use a PBL problem somewhere in between to help make the content more meaningful to the students. The more experience teachers gain with using PBL problems, the more comfortable, confident, and insightful they become about effectively placing problems throughout their typical instruction.

Further Considerations for K-1 Classrooms

- Teachers often supplement PBL units or lessons with additional relevant material. Supplemental activities and materials should be PBL in nature and should be embedded in the problem. Take care that they are not add-ons or tasks to be done alongside the problem.
- Five- and six-year-olds enjoy making up games with simple rules. These children do well in small-group activities, and it is best to avoid competitive activities. For example, one group's work should not be considered the "best" or the most correct. Fortunately, PBL focuses on multiple solutions and ideas rather than just correct answers.
- Much of the reality of five- and six-year-old worlds is rooted in stories and storybooks. Reading a story aloud is often an activity that helps the children connect the PBL problem to their own understanding of their role in the problem. Often, PBL teachers

will read half to two thirds of a related story and allow the children to finish the story with their own solutions and ideas. This approach avoids providing an "answer" to the PBL problem and encourages the students to solve the problem for themselves.

- Other popular activities include having the children draw their ideas, as in the *Oink!Oink!* example, or having the children make something that represents their ideas. In *Crunch, Munch, a Healthy Lunch,* the children made a menu and then prepared foods. For *The Terrible Toothache,* the children made models of a healthy mouth and an unhealthy mouth using white paper bags. In various other PBL problems, the children construct a birdfeeder, plant a garden, make a book of their ideas, and make natural dyes from food substances.

- Most of the activities teachers currently use are appropriate for use with PBL problems. The critical consideration is how to embed the problem in a PBL scenario so that it directly correlates with the intended objectives of the problem and directly aligns with the problem scenario. Activities should help the students move forward in their learning or discover something new that appears on the Need to Know list.

- Just as important as knowing when to use PBL problems and activities is knowing when not to use them. Five- and six-year-old children tend to run out of steam toward the end of the school day. Teachers are advised not to begin PBL problems in the last hour or so of the day. Remember that the PBL process is challenging to students and requires an energy level that is different from less active types of learning.

- Teachers should occasionally feel free to abandon the PBL process if they feel it is not working. This suggestion is not to abandon the idea of PBL completely but to determine why the process did not work well and then try it again at a later time. Consider the time of day, the children's energy level, the complexity of the PBL problem, how well the children could relate to the problem, and/or if additional resources were needed to make the problem effective.

- A concern that teachers often raise has to do with behavior issues when the children are working in small groups or without very specific direction. There is sometimes the assumption that children will take advantage of the small-group activity to misbehave or be "off task" or that they will not accomplish intended objectives without the usual type of guidance and direction. Experienced PBL teachers report that these concerns tend to be unfounded. Their experience is that using PBL actually eliminates some behavior problems. Many behavior problems occur when children are bored, distracted, or uninterested. Well-designed problems and appropriate facilitation will keep children engaged in the problem and focused on its outcome. The small groups allow for more even participation by children than the typical large-group classroom setting. When children are active participants in the outcome of their learning, they have little time or cause to be disruptive or "off task."

- An additional question is about the difference in the ability levels of students. This is a relevant issue for kindergartners, but most development issues do begin to resolve and even out during first grade. The key is to have an awareness of the range of abilities and to spread those through the small groups. For example, try to place a student with some reading or writing ability in each group. Place a creative student and a student who can articulate well in each group. Ensure that each group has a nurturing student and one who is willing to ask questions. Balancing the groups in these ways serves at least two purposes: It provides an equal distribution of the human resources, and it also gives developmentally younger students a chance to see their peers modeling different attributes.

- Teachers should bear in mind that PBL offers opportunities for cognitive, psychological, and emotional development in ways that many traditional approaches do not. However, PBL is not an answer to all educational issues. As questions arise about what to do when using PBL if certain issues do present themselves, teachers are reminded to consider what they are currently doing to manage those issues. Often, the strategies that are already in place will work very well alongside PBL instruction.

•♦3▲■

PBL and the 2-3 Classroom

Education would be so much more effective if its purpose were to ensure that by the time they leave school every boy and girl should know how much they don't know, and be imbued with a lifelong desire to know it.

—Sir William Haley (1901-1987)

Getting Started in the 2-3 Classroom

Problem selection for second- and third-grade students should be made with the developmental characteristics of these learners in mind. Children of this age are beginning to grow more independent. They are able to reason and verbalize their reasoning. They are able to search for needed information. Second and third graders are starting to enjoy making up stories rather than just hearing them.

Keeping those things in mind, PBL problems for these students are designed so the students seek out information and create an action plan for resolving the problem or completing an activity or project. These characteristics are demonstrated in several of the examples provided.

PBL problems are typically introduced by using an overhead transparency. A student volunteer is asked to read the problem aloud for the entire class. The teacher must avoid the temptation to do the reading. It is the students who need this reading practice.

Next, the class is divided into small groups of six to seven students each to make the lists of Facts, Need to Know, Action Plan, and Ideas/Solutions. The teacher should roam from group to group to assist the students in considering things that will lead them to the intended content or objectives of the problem. Once these lists are completed, there should be opportunity and support for researching the new information needed.

As students obtain new information, they should be prompted to revisit their lists and to revise them as needed. The acquisition of new information will change the list of Facts, create new Need to Know items, and affect the Action Plan and perhaps the Ideas/Solutions list. Students will need to be prompted to revisit their lists only a very few times, and then they will do so without being given the prompt. It is an essential step in the critical reasoning process, and it is important for the teacher to encourage this step until students integrate it into their own process.

At first, having several small groups of students working simultaneously feels slightly unnatural to many teachers. This kind of groupwork appears to have little or no order to it, and children do not often appear to be "on task." It is important to remember, however, that the students will get better at the process the more often they do it. Teachers should be patient in the early stages, and they will be rewarded by how much students are learning, producing, and demonstrating as a result of their groupwork. Teachers will also develop a rhythm for moving between the groups to monitor their progress and assist them as needed. This will also feel more natural with time and practice. Appendix A contains suggested "Facilitator Do" and "Facilitator Don't" behaviors that might be a useful reference while getting started.

It Looks Like This

The following example, *Hats of Courage,* is an example of a PBL problem that requires the students to do some planning as well as some research on their own. It is often used in third-grade classrooms, but it can be slightly modified for a second- or even a fourth-grade class. Although Darby is a fictional character in the problem, you will see how real she becomes to the students.

You know a little girl, Darby, who has leukemia. She is taking chemotherapy, and it has caused her hair to fall out. She would like a hat to wear so she will feel less self-conscious. Your group will need to design a hat for her that fits her personality.

What do you know and understand about Darby's illness?
What would be helpful to know about Darby?
How will you proceed?

The intended objectives of this problem are in vocabulary, health and healthy living, science, communication skills, math, and social studies.

After reading the problem aloud and together, the students go into their small groups and begin to identify the Facts. They then begin to determine the things they Need to Know. The list of Learning Issues that develops is typically both content oriented and process oriented. On the content side, the children need to know more about leukemia and cancer, chemotherapy, stages of this disease, and what is likely to happen to Darby during and after treatment. On the process side, the children want much more personal information about Darby, such as her favorite color, books, sport, games, foods, and television shows. They also begin to ask questions about ways to obtain this information. The students usually suggest meeting Darby, calling her on the phone, writing her a letter, and sending her an e-mail.

The students are likely to decide that they need more information before they can begin to design a hat. One class in particular decided that each group would make a list of the questions they wanted to ask Darby. Then the teacher would audiotape the questions as the group members read them aloud. The teacher would be responsible for getting the audiotape to Darby and for bringing her responses back to the class. In the meantime, the groups decided to look for the additional information they needed about the disease and treatment. The teacher had resources available including books, videotapes, and Web sites to assist them in their research.

In a couple of days, the teacher brought in Darby's responses to the audiotaped questions. The teacher created the responses herself for this fictional character and provided a copy of the responses to each group. The children felt they were ready to design their hats, but the teacher first had them revisit their lists to make certain they had all the information they needed and to include any new information they had found.

The groups did revise their lists, and the new Need to Know list included things such as what materials were available for making a hat; whether they had money to spend on the hat and, if so, how much; and when they should give the hat to Darby. Notice that the children assumed they would make and give a hat to Darby even though the original problem was only to design a hat. This assumption is consistent with the fact that other children, especially friends, are becoming more important to third graders. In this class, when the teacher realized that the children intended to actually make a hat rather than just design one, she accommodated them in these ways.

The teacher first had the children identify what resources were available for making a hat. Their design needed to include these things, or else they would have to make a plan for obtaining the additional materials, such as bringing them from home. The teacher herself purchased five generic children's caps (these were about $3 each) and gave one to each group. There were two denim baseball caps, two white baseball caps, and a khaki floppy hat. Once each group received its hat, the children planned their design and then how to actually make the hat look like the design.

Once the hats were completed, the teacher contacted the local children's hospital and described what her class had done and would like to donate. A pediatric oncologist identified a 9-year-old patient who had indeed lost her hair during treatment and was due back in the hospital soon. The teacher made arrangements to visit this patient personally and to have her choose a hat from the five created by the class. The other four hats were then left in the clinic area for the staff to distribute to other patients. The teacher also made arrangements to have her visit to the little girl videotaped so she could show the students back in her class who received the hat.

This turned out to be a powerful character education lesson as the children viewed the videotape. They saw a little girl about their own age in her hospital bed, a little girl who cried as she thanked them on tape for their thoughtfulness. The students also heard the mother's voice fill with emotion as she thanked the children, too.

This example illustrates how encompassing a PBL problem can be and how one problem can extend over a period of several days. The children addressed science and health learning issues regarding the disease. They did mathematics equations concerning the cost of a hat and materials. They discussed healthy living in terms of preventing diseases and, finally, how to improve the quality of life of someone who may be suffering as the result of a disease. The children were also required to develop and execute a plan for designing an appropriate hat, based on personal information about the patient. In this case, the teacher chose to make the problem very real to the students by videotaping the delivery of the hat to a real patient.

This also demonstrates the process for introducing a PBL problem in the Grade 2 or 3 classroom and provides some ideas about what to anticipate from the students. It illustrates that the problems are designed with very intentional content objectives and that often, quite significant unintentional content objectives present themselves. This example also shows the ways in which PBL allows students to demonstrate what they already know and how they are already thinking critically.

More Examples

Teachers who are comfortable with creating PBL problems "on their feet" often turn students' questions about one thing or another into a PBL problem. However, most teachers prefer to look over prepared problems, anticipate the resources the students may need, set up related activities, and have a clear sense of the directions in which they will guide the problem.

As mentioned in Chapter 2, there are two primary sources for prepared problems. One is problems developed by other PBL teachers. Many schools keep a file of these. Another source is to prepare one's own problems. Specific information about authoring your own problems is provided in the last chapter. In the meantime, here are two more examples of PBL problem scenarios that have been used successfully in classrooms. The first example is a problem that is quite focused. The second example is slightly more open ended: The teacher may direct the students in one direction or another or let the students self-direct. Of course, for each example and others in the book, teachers will use the outline given in Table 1.1 (PBL Process), emphasizing those areas the teacher feels are most important for a particular lesson.

The following problem is an example that can be customized by region or state; this qualifies as a focused PBL problem. *The Cherokee Museum* has these objectives: Native American history, North Carolina history, and cultural diversity. This problem can easily be adapted to focus students on the desired geographic region by simply changing the criteria of the exhibit. The scenario for this problem is as follows:

> Your class has been selected to help prepare a Cherokee exhibit for the opening of the Native American wing of the Natural Science Museum. Your class can choose any items that truly represent the Cherokee culture.

This problem scenario continues after the students have developed their lists of Facts and items they Need to Know.

The museum curator has informed us that we have 100 square feet for the exhibit. It is intended for the general public to appreciate.

The students research to determine items that are appropriate to include. They design the exhibit and make some of the things they wish to display. The class is divided into small groups, and each group is expected to present their exhibit design to the class upon completion. The class will then combine their designs to create the exhibit. After each group presents its exhibit design to the class, this additional scenario is given to the class:

Combining your exhibit items requires more space than has been allotted. The curator asks that you limit your exhibit to six items. Each group may now make recommendations about which items to include. Be prepared to defend your selections.

Typically, the children do not initially heed the space limitation set out in the problem. Now they must come back to it and do measurements and often trace the space off in some way on the classroom floor to determine its size. The students must now also be prepared to defend their selections by demonstrating the reasoning used to include those items.

The next example, *Creepy, Crawly Caterpillars,* is more open ended and may be used to introduce a unit on animal life cycles and the needs of living organisms. Here is the problem scenario:

You are an entomologist (bug expert). You are called in to help rid an area of very hungry caterpillars that are devouring local gardens and trees. Although you understand why the callers are concerned, you feel you must warn them about killing off too many insects.

What do you know about caterpillars?
What do you need to know about caterpillars and other insects?
What options exist besides exterminating the caterpillars?

The students are usually aware that caterpillars turn into butterflies, but they are usually not aware that there are other life stages as well. They may explore this concept focusing on caterpillars and then extend the concept to other insects. At this time, they may discover that there are helpful and harmful aspects to the presence of different insects.

The students may have some knowledge of the use of pesticides to control insects in gardens. This can lead to lessons on environmental harmony, quality of soil for gardening, and other ways to control the insect population. Students may discuss the benefits of garden production versus the benefits of the insects' presence.

The children might also consider a world without butterflies in terms of the aesthetics of certain creatures and how they otherwise contribute to the environment. Of course, this conversation can also be extended to a variety of insects.

This PBL problem can easily be used to engage the students in all of these learning areas or only in selected ones. If the teacher prefers to focus on one area rather than others, she simply prompts the children in that direction by asking the questions that lead the children into those learning areas.

Types of PBL Problems

Most PBL problems afford the teacher choices. Once the teacher becomes familiar with the rhythm and flow of different types of problems, selection becomes easier. Predictability in how children will respond to the problems also increases. As a teacher develops this level of experience and comfort with PBL, it is important to remember that broad problems with many potential learning issues are initially more difficult to facilitate and are typically more challenging to the students. Focused problems generally provide the children with a clearer direction for their learning.

An example of each type of problem is given here to illustrate the differences.

Problem 1. Samuel, Sarah, and You
(An Open-Ended Problem)

The scenario is:

Last night you dreamed that you were working at your computer. Suddenly you are sucked into the monitor. You tumble through time and space and find yourself in the middle of the street on a cold day. You look around for anyone you know, but no one is there. You see people dressed differently. You are scared and feel lost.

A boy and girl approach you, looking as if they want to help. The boy says his name is Samuel and tells you that the girl is Sarah, his sister. They invite you to come home with them and stay until you figure out how to get home.

Samuel and Sarah remind you of pictures you have seen of Pilgrims. You are pretty sure that is the time you have arrived in during your trip. You are now more curious than scared and are interested to see how Samuel, Sarah, and their family live.

What do you already know about how Pilgrims lived?
What questions will you ask Samuel and Sarah?
Plan how you will tell everyone at home about what you
   learn.

Students prepare their lists and begin to plan how they will find the information on their Need to Know list. The problem references several resources including books about Pilgrim children, a video on colonial life for children, and Internet resources. Children may be reminded of the facts about colonial life by reading *Samuel Eaton's Day* and *Sarah Morton's Day*. These or similar stories prompt the students to recall the differences between modern life and colonial life.

The learning areas for this problem may include geography to understand how the climate affected colonial life. Social studies objectives include the historical concepts of the settlers' arriving here in unfamiliar territory and the adjustments they made. The historical concept of progress and development is also a possibility. Math may be a learning issue as incomes and budgets are considered in comparing colonial times to modern times. How crops were grown and sold or how other commerce influenced colonial life might be learning topics. This type of PBL problem is rich with possibilities for student learning. Teachers may choose to have this type of problem occur over several weeks to include many of the areas, or they may choose to focus the children on fewer topics.

The following example is a PBL problem that would occur over a much briefer time and that is quite focused to a specific learning area.

Problem 2. Swings 'n' Things (A More Focused Problem)

The scenario is:

> Our school is building a new playground. Our class has been asked to submit a proposal or model of the ideal playground to the principal. The PTA fund-raiser this year will give $15,000 to build the playground.

The students list the facts they know and then the things they would like to know. Usually they will need to know where the playground will be located, how large it will be, and what playground equipment costs. The teacher should be prepared to provide this information to the students. The location and size of the playground is flexible, depending on the school and playground. Equipment catalogs or Internet sites give the students an idea of the expenses involved.

The teacher may then prompt the children to consider visiting the playground site and measuring areas for the equipment layout. If safety issues have not been mentioned, he or she will want to prompt the students to consider these. What age children will be using the playground and the equipment? How many children might use the area at the same time? What precautions can be made to ensure the safety of students on the playground and on the equipment?

Different resources are appropriate for addressing these questions. The principal might be invited to the class to talk about safety on the playground. A parent experienced in construction could be invited to discuss equipment placement and how much space to allot to ensure safety. A representative from the city or county Parks and Recreation Department could visit to discuss playground design and recommend equipment preferences.

A good activity for this problem is to have each student group draw their design to scale. They can provide a narrative to demonstrate why their design is the most desirable. Each group might then present their design to the class and perhaps to the principal as well.

This problem is quite focused and can be done in a couple of mornings or afternoons.

Further Considerations for 2-3 Classrooms

- Second and third graders are ready to begin developing and executing plans of their own. Effective PBL problems for this age group will incorporate the opportunity for students to do this.
- These students are also developing an awareness of their own independence and becoming considerate of others. This is a good time to have cooperative learning opportunities and service learning lessons and to have these students work in groups or teams.
- Second and third graders have also developed their fine-motor skills to a level that allows them to build models and construct projects. Problems often include the chance for students to do this in order to demonstrate their understanding, as in the examples *The Cherokee Museum* and *Hats of Courage*. In other PBL problems, the children might plant a garden, design and make a brochure, or make a videotape of a newscast.
- Most of the activities teachers currently use are appropriate for PBL problems. The critical consideration is how to integrate the project or activity in a PBL scenario so that it directly correlates with the intended objectives of the problem and directly aligns with the problem scenario. Activities should help the students move forward in their learning or discover something new that appears on the Need to Know list.
- Teachers often supplement PBL units or lessons with additional relevant material. Supplemental activities and materials might be PBL in nature but should always be directly aligned with the problem.

- Just as important as knowing when to use PBL problems and activities is knowing when not to use them. Teachers are advised not to begin PBL problems in the last hour or so of the day. Remember that the PBL process is challenging to students and requires an energy level that is different from less active types of learning.

- Teachers should feel free to retreat from the PBL process if they feel it is not working. This suggestion is not to abandon the idea of PBL completely but to determine why the process did not work well and then try it again at a later time. Consider the time of day, the students' energy level, the complexity of the PBL problem, how well the children could relate to the problem, and/or if additional resources were needed to make the problem effective. Remember, PBL is just one of several methods in a teacher's repertoire.

- A concern that teachers often raise has to do with behavior issues when the children are working in small groups or without very specific direction. There is sometimes the assumption that children will take advantage of the small-group activity to misbehave or be "off task" or that they will not accomplish intended objectives without the usual type of guidance and direction. Experienced PBL teachers report that these concerns tend to be unfounded. Their experience is that using PBL actually eliminates some behavior problems. Many behavior problems occur when children are bored, distracted, or uninterested. Well-designed problems and appropriate teacher help will keep children engaged in the problem and focused on its outcome. The small groups allow for more even participation by children than the typical large-group classroom setting. When children are active participants in the outcome of their learning, they have little time or cause to be disruptive or "off task."

- Teachers should bear in mind that PBL offers opportunities for cognitive, psychological, and emotional development in ways that many traditional approaches do not. However, PBL is not an answer to all educational issues. As questions arise about what to do when using PBL if certain issues do present themselves, teachers are reminded to consider what they are currently doing to manage those issues. Often, the strategies that are already in place will work very well alongside PBL instruction.

●◆4▲■

PBL and the 4-6 Classroom

An education isn't how much you have committed to
memory, or even how much you know. It's being able to dif-
ferentiate between what you do know and what you don't.

—Anatole France (1844-1924)

Getting Started
in the 4-6 Classroom

Fourth- through sixth-grade children are more capable of understanding concepts, and the PBL problems selected should present this opportunity to them. This age group can also focus
attention for longer periods, and children of this age enjoy talking through problems to solve them. They are beginning to understand and consider the opinions of others as an influence in their
decision making. Thus, problem selection for these students cap-
italizes on their willingness to engage in the more mature PBL
problem.

PBL problems can be introduced by using an overhead transparency, providing the students a written copy, or both. A student volunteer is asked to read the problem aloud for the entire class.

The class is divided into small groups of six or seven students each to make the lists of Facts, Need to Know, Action Plan, and Ideas/Solutions. The teacher roams from group to group to prompt the students to consider things that will lead them to the desired content or objectives of the problem. Once these lists are completed, the students should begin researching the new information needed.

After students have gathered new information, they need to revisit their lists and revise them as needed. New information will change the list of Facts, generate new Need to Know items, and affect the Action Plan and perhaps the Ideas/Solutions list. Students will need to be prompted to revisit their lists only a very few times, and then they will do so independent of the prompt. This is an essential step in the critical reasoning process, and it is important for the teacher to encourage this step until students integrate it into their own process.

Initially, working with several small groups of students feels slightly unnatural to many teachers. Students do not always appear to be "on task." The students will get better at the process the more often they do it. Teachers will need patience in the early stages, and they will be rewarded by how much students are learning, producing, and demonstrating as a result of their group-work. Teachers will also develop a rhythm for moving among the groups to monitor progress and guide the students. Appendix A contains suggested "Facilitator Do" and "Facilitator Don't" behaviors that might be a useful reference while getting started.

Problem Examples

Two examples of PBL problems are given here. More problem examples appropriate for these grade levels may be found in Appendix B.

The following example, *Patty O'Design,* is a PBL problem that appeals to the interest these students have in expressing their individualism and in working out a solution. It was designed for use in a sixth-grade classroom, but the objectives can be modified for fourth or fifth graders.

You are employed as a landscape architect. You work on the design team, and your group receives this letter:

Smith-Jones Landscaping Design, Inc.
1575 East Forsyth Boulevard

Dear Sir or Madam:

We are interested in adding a patio to our house. We have decided that we would like to use as much as possible of the 20-foot by 20-foot area directly behind our house for a patio shaped in a nontraditional design. We would like for you to submit two designs with specifications so that we can choose the one we like better. Please be aware that we want to use at least 340 square feet of the available area for the patio.

We have read your brochure and enclosed the $200 design fee. We appreciate your guaranteed delivery date of 1 week.

Sincerely,

Ian and Patty O'Brien

What would be helpful to know before you begin your design?
How will this information help you?
What will you do next?

The intended objectives of this problem are using calculations and calculators, practicing computation, understanding similar figures, learning terminology and vocabulary, investigating open-ended problems, formulating questions, extending problem-solving situations, and developing communication skills.

The problem is read within the large group, and then the students go into their small groups. They first identify the Facts. Then they begin to determine the things they Need to Know. The list of Learning Issues that develops usually contains questions that are content related and others that are process related. Regarding content, the students need to know more about measuring the space, figuring the square footage, and what is meant by nontraditional. The process issues relate more to the preferences of the clients about design, materials, special features, and the budget for the project. They usually decide that they will have to communicate in some way with this couple before they can proceed.

The teacher can decide how this information will be provided for the students. One teacher had "the couple" come to her class to answer questions. In this case, "the couple" were parent volunteers from a different grade level, so they were somewhat anonymous to the class. The visit was followed up with a letter from the couple to document their requests. The follow-up letter is provided in the case materials and can be distributed after the students have composed a letter to the couple, sent an e-mail, or left a phone message. The letter that one teacher provided is on the next page.

The problem has pictures included to represent the types of designs the O'Briens saw on their vacation. Teachers who wish to use this problem can provide similar examples from patio design catalogs, home improvement catalogs, or downloaded designs from an Internet Web site.

The students work in their small groups to create patio designs that fulfill the criteria given to them in the problem. Most student groups do research to help them understand the definitions and calculations involved in determining perimeter measurements and area. They develop a concept of nontraditional design and apply it to their own ideas. It is helpful for the students to have graph paper to sketch their initial plans. One successful activity has been to have the students go into the school yard with measuring tools and string to lay out their design.

Smith-Jones Landscaping Design, Inc.
1575 East Forsyth Boulevard

Dear Sir or Madam:

This letter is to inform you of the modifications we would like to add to our original instructions in regard to your company's designing a patio for us.

Looking back on our vacation photos of our trip out West last year, we were reminded of some creative yet beautiful patios we saw. We would like for you to make sure that your designs for our patio have the following features:

- We would like two areas for flowers on the sides of the patio that are adjacent to the house. Please use only about 70% of patio footage for the flower areas; then on each side extending from the house out to the yard, use about 80%.
- A small area in the center of the patio for flowers (this area should be in the same geometric shape as the patio design and about 10% of the entire patio size).

Again, thank you very much for your cooperation and understanding in this matter. We eagerly await your designs.

Sincerely yours,

Ian and Patty O'Brien

This problem is usually completed in 3 to 4 days. At some point over the course of the several days, students will need to revisit their original lists to see if the Facts have changed or if new Need to Know items have emerged. Finally, each group presents its finished design in a poster display. The class as a whole is then encouraged to come to a consensus about the best design, in consideration of the couple's criteria. Students must demonstrate their reasoning and understanding of the concepts in order to reach this consensus.

This example illustrates how a PBL problem can address very specific learning objectives, such as measurement and calculations, while still integrating other learning areas very effectively. It also provides some insight into how problem introduction occurs in fourth- through sixth-grade classrooms and what to expect from the students.

A few teachers are comfortable creating PBL problems "on their feet," using students' questions to develop a possible scenario and proceeding from there. However, most teachers prefer to look over prepared problems, anticipate the resources the students may need, set up related activities, and have a clear sense of the directions in which they will guide the problem and the students.

As indicated in Chapter 2, there are two primary sources for prepared problems. One of these is the problems developed by other PBL teachers. Many schools keep a file of these. Another source is to prepare one's own problems. Specific information about authoring your own problems is provided in the last chapter. In the meantime, here is another example of a PBL problem scenario that has been used successfully in Grades 4 to 6. Of course, for this example and others in the book, teachers will use the outline given in Table 1.1 (PBL Process), emphasizing those areas the teacher feels are most important for a particular lesson.

The following problem appeals to students in this age group because of its futuristic setting and the opportunity for students to create the rules for a game. The scenario is called *Moonball.*

You have been elected commissioner of the newly formed Moon Basketball Association (MBA). It is your job, along with your expert advisers, to establish league playing rules at the newly constructed moon base. Changes in the rules and regulations are necessary now because of the different playing conditions. Your group has been asked to provide an explanation of why the changes you recommend are necessary. (For information on basketball rules, see the National Collegiate Athletic Association [NCAA] Web site at www.ncaabasketball.net/rulebook.asp)

> What would be helpful to know before you begin to establish
>   new rules?
> How will this information help you?
> What will you do next?

The primary objective of this problem is for students to investigate gravity as a universal force. The breadth and depth to which the students pursue this exploration will be determined by their grade level, curriculum objectives, and how the teacher guides the development of their Need to Know list.

The students are provided with some resources such as an official rule book for basketball, usually available from a high school coach or athletic director, and other game books that might be available through the physical education department. Science textbooks, especially earth science textbooks, with a section on gravity are helpful, and bookmarked Internet resources may be supplied.

After completing the appropriate research, students then design the rules they will recommend for the game of Moonball. The teacher can decide how the student groups will communicate their new rules and regulations to the rest of the class. Student groups may develop a handbook, create a poster, or do a class presentation to share their recommendations. The teacher is reminded to have a mechanism in place that requires the students to explain why the changes they make are necessary to adapt the game to different atmospheric conditions. Teachers can extend the learning by adding the following to the problem:

> If you were to expand this league to an interplanetary league,
> what locations would you choose, and what different changes
> would you make for these new locations?

This optional addition to the problem gives the students a chance to demonstrate their understanding of the concepts explored, their ability to apply that understanding, and, at the same time, to engage in new learning as they explore atmospheric conditions of other planets.

Further Considerations
for 4-6 Classrooms

- A PBL problem may be used to introduce a unit of study or to wrap up a unit, or it may be dispersed throughout instruction. The two previous PBL problems demonstrate examples of a focused design and a more open-ended design, respectively. The length of time a teacher chooses to use a PBL problem can be based on the problem itself, the maturity of the students, and how the teacher chooses to guide the problem.

- As a teacher develops the ability to predict how students will respond to different types of PBL problems, problem selection becomes easier. Remember that broad problems with many potential learning issues are initially more difficult to facilitate and are typically more challenging to the students. Focused problems generally provide the children a clearer direction for their learning.

- Students in Grades 4 to 6 are attracted to problem-solving activities. The use of multiple scenarios within a PBL problem is recommended for this age group, as doing so keeps the problem flowing and sustains the interest of the students.

- Fourth through sixth graders are capable of doing relatively in-depth independent research. It is particularly helpful to provide these students with a variety of resources and let them select the most appropriate or appealing. This increases their familiarity with the range of possible resources and gives them practice in selecting the best resource for the needed information.

- Intellectually, these students are becoming more interested in how-to projects. They can be especially engaged in PBL problems that require them to construct models, blueprints, or detailed drawings of their solutions. For example, in the *Patty O'Design* problem, the students enjoy outlining their design on the school grounds with stakes and string. In the *Moonball* example, the students often create a league manual detailing the new rules.

- Teachers frequently have classroom activities already developed that they know to be instructional and successful. Such activities can still be used to supplement PBL units or lessons. Supplemental activities and materials should be PBL in nature and should be directly aligned with the problem.

- Effective PBL problems for this age group often incorporate the opportunity for students to teach other students. They may develop lessons that align with the problem and give the information to the other small groups within their own class. Another successful plan for this strategy is to create a problem that requires these students to design and deliver areas of instruction to younger students in other classrooms. The older students, sixth graders especially, enjoy this activity, and the younger children in other classrooms like the interaction.

- These students are continuing to develop an awareness of their own independence and consideration of others. This is a good time for cooperative learning opportunities and service learning lessons; consider having these students demonstrate service in a culminating activity aligned with the PBL problem.

- Most of the activities teachers currently use are appropriate for use with PBL problems. The critical consideration is how to integrate the project or activity in a PBL scenario so that it correlates with the intended objectives of the problem and directly aligns with the problem scenario. Activities should help the students to achieve better understanding in their learning or to discover something new that appears on the Need to Know list.

- Just as important as knowing when to use PBL problems and activities is knowing when not to use them. Teachers are advised not to begin PBL problems in the last hour or so of the day. Remember that the PBL process is challenging to students and requires an energy level that is different from less active types of learning. Also, you may need some extra time for clarification of issues that come up with more mature PBL problems.

- Teachers should occasionally feel free to retreat from the PBL process if they feel it is not working. This suggestion is not to abandon the idea of PBL completely but to determine why the process did not work well and then to try it again at a later time. Consider the time of day, the students' energy level, the complexity of the PBL problem, how well the students could relate to the problem, and/or if additional resources were needed to make the problem effective.

- A concern that teachers often raise has to do with behavior issues when students are working in small groups or without very specific direction. There is sometimes the assumption that students will take advantage of the small-group activity to misbehave or be "off task" or that they will not accomplish intended objectives without the usual type of guidance and direction. Experienced PBL teachers report that these concerns tend to be unfounded. In their experience, using PBL actually eliminates some behavior problems. Many behavior problems occur when students are bored, distracted, or uninterested. Students in the fourth- through sixth-grade groups are also becoming more concerned with peer pressure and will want to perform in their groups in ways that are appreciated. Well-designed problems and appropriate facilitation will keep students engaged in the problem and focused on its outcome. The design and facilitation are the keys here. PBL does require careful preparation and active coaching. The small groups allow for more even participation by students than the typical large-group classroom setting. When students are active participants in the direction and outcome of their learning, they have little time or cause to be disruptive or "off task."

- Teachers should bear in mind that PBL offers opportunities for cognitive, psychological, and emotional development in ways that many traditional approaches do not. However, PBL is not an answer to all educational issues. As questions arise about what to do when using PBL if certain issues do present themselves, teachers are reminded to consider what they are currently doing to manage those issues. Often, the strategies that are already in place will work very well alongside PBL instruction.

●◆5▲■

PBL and the 7-8 Classroom

Getting things done is not always what is most important. There is value in allowing others to learn, even if the task is not accomplished as quickly, efficiently or effectively.

—R. D. Clyde

Getting Started in the 7-8 Classroom

Choosing effective PBL problems for these students should acknowledge that they enjoy being challenged. As this age group starts to exercise more and more independence from adults, they appreciate the opportunity to work things out for themselves. These students are developmentally ready not just to access new information but also to determine its relevance and to apply it. Selected PBL problems should allow ample opportunity for students to demonstrate their growing and more mature abilities.

Seventh and eighth graders typically experience a new level of stress that accompanies this developmental stage. Evidence indicates that peer support, active decision making, and planning help reduce the stress levels these students often feel. The dynamics and activities of PBL are very effective in reducing stress among these students. Seventh- and eighth-grade students can tackle PBL problems that are longer in duration, richer in content, and more complex in problem-solving challenges.

The options for introducing PBL problems can be varied for seventh and eighth graders. Using an overhead transparency or providing the students a written copy of the problem are still standard strategies. Another strategy is to have students keep a notebook of PBL problems. The notebooks double as learning journals and increase students' organizational skills. A written copy of the problem is put into the notebook, and the students document the learning issues to be pursued. The notebook is also a repository for newly acquired information and for new thoughts or ideas about problem resolution. If a problem is designed to last over many class periods or even several weeks, the notebooks support the students in organizing material and monitoring their own progress as they work through the problem components. These notebooks can become part of the assessment process as well.

As in the younger grades, the class is divided into small groups of six or seven students. Teachers will need to pay more attention to group composition now than at the earlier grade levels. Groups should be balanced for academic talent, extroversion and introversion characteristics, and the avoidance of cliques within the group. Next, the groups will make the lists of Facts, Need to Know, Action Plan, and Ideas/Solutions. The teacher moves from group to group to be certain that the students consider things that will lead them to the intended content or objectives of the problem. Seventh and eighth graders should include in their Action Plan a list of potential resources for the research they are about to begin—a list that will be longer than what younger students would produce. This list will contain many possibilities, only some of which will be used. These students should start to develop the skills to discern credible sources of information, to effectively and efficiently access those sources, and to synthesize information from various sources.

Students will need to revisit their lists often and to revise them as needed. As they bring new information to the problem, the lists of Facts, Need to Know, Action Plan, and perhaps the Ideas/Solutions list will change to reflect the reality that students know and understand additional content. Students should be prompted to revisit their lists until they do so independent of the prompt. This is an essential step in the critical reasoning process, and it is important for the teacher to ensure that it becomes integrated into the process.

Monitoring and prompting several small groups of students simultaneously feels slightly unnatural to many teachers. This kind of groupwork can appear quite chaotic, it has the tendency to get loud, and students do not always appear to be "on task." The students will get better at the process and more organized in their approach to problems the more often they do it. Of course, problems will vanish rather quickly if students have had PBL experience in earlier grades. However, if that is not the case, teachers will need patience as they gain experience introducing PBL, and they will be rewarded by how much students are learning, producing, and demonstrating as a result of their groupwork. Teachers will also develop a rhythm for moving among the groups to monitor progress and guide the students as needed. Appendix A contains suggested "Facilitator Do" and "Facilitator Don't" behaviors that might be useful references while getting started.

Problem Examples

Here are two examples of PBL problems for these older students. Additional PBL problems appropriate for these grade levels can be found in Appendix B.

The first example, *Teresa and Carl,* appeals to these students because it presents a mystery to be solved, is a story line about a couple (an interest they are developing), and puts them in a career role that is unfamiliar but intriguing. It was designed for use in a seventh-grade classroom, but the objectives can be easily modified for use with eighth graders.

You are a genetics counselor. You have an appointment with new clients today, Teresa and Carl. They are engaged to be married and have come to you with this concern:

At their engagement party, Teresa and Carl both overheard different family members talking about relatives with "the disease." They never overheard the name of the disease, but they did hear that Teresa's father and maternal aunt both have the illness. Carl overheard that his uncle and maternal grandmother have it as well. The symptoms that they heard described include intense pain in different parts of the body, fatigue, and shortness of breath.

Because it seemed like such a sensitive subject to those discussing it, Teresa and Carl were reluctant to ask their family members any additional questions. Instead, they have come to you for information about whether they may have already inherited the disease. They also want to know if they could pass it along to their own children, even if they show no signs of the illness.

What additional information would you like to have?

How will this information help you?

What will you do next?

The intended objectives of this problem include understanding genetic diseases and symptoms, sex-linked diseases, heterozygous versus homozygous traits, DNA, chromosomes, mitosis, meiosis, and the role of a genetics counselor.

The problem may be read within the large group or distributed to students already in their small groups. Students should first identify the Facts as given to them. They then will develop their lists of Learning Issues or Need to Know items. The list of Learning Issues usually contains questions about inherited diseases, detecting existing disease, predicting the effect of parental diseases on children, and what symptoms reveal about certain diseases. Students should also question the role of the genetics counselor, but that usually comes up later in the problem. Typically, students first want to solve this mystery and then to determine how best to advise Teresa and Carl and exactly what their role is in doing so.

Students will often indicate the need to know something about the couple's background, such as age and ethnicity. Some teachers choose simply to provide this information to the students when asked. Other teachers have provided the students with a set of photographs of what the couple might look like. Photographs are usually taken from a magazine and have included African American couples or couples with characteristics that might, for instance, suggest Jewish heritage or couples with Nordic features. The students do not know with certainty at this stage which couple is actually Teresa and Carl.

The groups usually discover early in their research that they will need blood samples from Teresa and Carl. The results of the blood tests are included in this problem. The teacher distributes this information to each group as they identify the need to know it. Once this information is given to the students, they will need to revise their lists. They will have a lot of new learning issues regarding the information in the blood test report. Students will need to determine, again, how they will find the kind of information that they need to move forward with resolving the problem.

Through their research efforts, the students will eventually rule out all potential diseases except sickle-cell anemia. They must then determine how to counsel Teresa and Carl regarding their own health and their question about having children.

This problem is designed to last approximately 1 week using a 50-minute class period each day. The problem often concludes with students from each group role-playing the counsel they give to Teresa and Carl. Teachers encourage the groups to include poster graphics to help the couple understand their situation. Two students in the group take on the roles of the couple, one becomes the genetics counselor, and the other group members are brought in as expert consultants to assist in the explanation of the scientific data to the couple. Not only do students enjoy this component, but the learning continues, as the different groups often explain additional factors that may not have been pursued across all groups.

As in the preceding problem, the complexity of problems that will engage seventh and eighth graders usually requires more preparation than is necessary with younger students. Teachers will want to anticipate the resources the students may need, set up related activities and labs, and have a distinct sense of the directions in which they will guide the problem and the students.

As mentioned in Chapter 2, there are two primary sources for prepared problems. One of those sources is problems developed by other PBL teachers. Many schools keep a file of these. Another source is to prepare one's own problems. Specific information about authoring your own problems is provided in the last chapter. In the meantime, here is another example of a PBL problem scenario that has been used successfully in seventh- and eighth-grade classrooms. Of course, as usual, teachers will use the outline in Table 1.1 (PBL Process), emphasizing those areas the teacher feels are most important for a particular lesson.

This next PBL problem appeals to seventh and eighth graders largely because it puts them in control of a design that is always relegated to an adult authority figure. In this case, that adult is typically a coach. These students may have had some experience with a coach themselves, may have watched sports and criticized coaches' decisions, or may have heard their parents do the same. The problem is called *Player's Choice*.

> You are the statistician for a new National Basketball Association (NBA) team. Your owner has asked you to analyze the data of the team's 15 players. You are then to advise the owner about who you think would be the five best STARTING LINEUP players for the team this season. The team owner has asked that you provide graphic presentations along with your recommendations.
>
> > What would be helpful to know about each player?
> > How will this information help you?
> > What will you do next?

The objectives for this problem include understanding averaging or finding the mean, ratio/percentage, rounding, graphing, statistical analysis, and applying statistics to a game strategy.

The students are given statistical information about each of the players. The teachers who developed this problem used the existing statistics of the top 15 NBA players, omitting player names. This information can be obtained from a number of sports-oriented Web sites. The one used for this problem contains the statistical information for the top 50 NBA players. The Web site address is www.nba.com, and it features a link to the players' statistics. For this problem, the statistics are provided on 15 different attributes, such as number of games played, field goals attempted and made, 3-point goals attempted and made, free throws attempted and made, assists, offensive rebounds, and defensive rebounds. As the students are analyzing this information, they receive this update from the owner:

> Player 6 has just been placed on suspension for failing a drug test. The owner needs an update on Player 6's average number of points. He also asks for a visual presentation from the coach by next week to present to the stockholders to justify keeping Player 6 on the team. The coach needs your help to prepare this information.

Another update may be provided to students as they continue to work on their analysis.

> Player 11 has just been traded. You are to choose a new player to recommend to the owner as a replacement. You are limited to a pool of free agents who are currently available midseason.

Students are then given the information available on the pool of free agents. This information contains the same sort of statistical data they have for the original 15 players.

Each group will recommend their "dream team" in a presentation at the conclusion of the problem. They must defend the choices they have made and use their statistical analysis to support their selections. They must also apply this information to an appropriate game strategy given the lineup they are recommending.

At the conclusion of all the presentations, the teacher reveals the identities of the professional players whose statistics were used. Students are often amazed at whom they eliminated from their "dream team" and at whom they retained. There is a powerful lesson in this component as students realize the value and the limitations of using statistical analysis alone. Teachers often use this opportunity to relate the interpretation of statistics to other areas of the students' lives. Nearly every student can think of a sentence they have overheard indicating that "Statistics show . . . ." Students gain insight about understanding, trusting, and questioning the use of statistical information in decision making. They learn that there may be other factors such as leadership, cooperation, or inspiration that play a role in determining the starting team.

Further Considerations for 7-8 Classrooms

- A PBL problem may be used to introduce or wrap up a unit of study, or it may be dispersed throughout instruction. The length of time a teacher chooses to use a PBL problem can be based on the problem itself, the maturity of the students, and on how the teacher chooses to guide the problem. The two PBL problems in this chapter demonstrate the possible use of additional information to manipulate the length and complexity of a problem.

- As a teacher develops the ability to predict how students will respond to different types of PBL problems, problem selection becomes easier. Remember that broad problems with many potential learning issues are initially more difficult to facilitate but are typically more challenging to the students. Focused problems generally provide the students a clearer direction for their learning and achieve very specific learning objectives.

- Seventh- and eighth-grade students are attracted to PBL problems that give them the opportunity to demonstrate how they would handle a problem independent of adult decision makers. Using multiple scenarios or new information within a PBL problem helps these students gain the insight that problems are rarely as straightforward as they may seem on the surface. Teachers should encourage students to reflect on and express how the new information affected their way of thinking about a problem.

- Students in the seventh and eighth grades are capable of doing in-depth independent research. It is important that they experience a variety of information sources that they identify. Among these sources, they should begin to discern how to determine credibility. This is especially true in the case of Internet sites. It becomes increasingly important that students be able to distinguish a reliable Web-based resource from those that might provide questionable information.

- These students are becoming more interested in what their futures as adults might hold. They may be considering college, careers, and romantic relationships in ways that are new to them. They can be especially engaged in PBL problems that require them to explore these different dimensions of maturing. For example, in the case of Teresa and Carl, it is not such a stretch for the students to consider themselves part of an engaged couple contemplating having children one day.

- As mentioned in Chapter 4, and just as true for these students, effective PBL problems for this age group often incorporate the opportunity for students to teach other students. They may develop lessons that align with the problem and give the information to the other small groups within their own class. Another successful plan for this strategy is to create a problem in which these students design and deliver areas of instruction to younger students in other classrooms. These older students especially enjoy this activity, and the younger children in other classrooms like this interaction.

- Seventh and eighth graders are developing a higher awareness of their own independence and a desire to be more responsible. This is a good time to use PBL problems that include service learning projects in the school and community, ethical issues, and current events that have a controversial dimension.

- Most of the labs and activities teachers currently use are appropriate for use with PBL problems. The critical consideration is how to integrate the project or activity in a PBL scenario so that it correlates with the intended objectives of the problem and directly aligns with the problem scenario. Laboratory exercises and other activities should help the students achieve better understanding in their learning or discover something new that appears on the Need to Know list.

- Teachers, as mentioned in earlier chapters, should occasionally feel free to retreat from the PBL process if they feel it is not working. It is important to determine why the process did not work well and then try it again at a later time. Consider the time of day, the students' energy level, the complexity of the PBL problem, how well the students could relate to the problem, and/or if additional resources were needed to make the problem effective.

- A concern that teachers often raise has to do with behavior issues when students are working in small groups or without very specific direction. There is sometimes the assumption that students will take advantage of the small-group activity to socialize or be "off task" or that they will not accomplish intended objectives without the usual type of guidance and direction. Experienced PBL teachers report that these concerns tend to be unfounded. In their experience, using PBL actually eliminates some behavior problems. Many behavior problems occur when students are bored, distracted, or uninterested. Students in the seventh- and eighth-grade age groups are also becoming more concerned with peer pressure and will want to perform in their groups in ways that are appreciated. Well-designed problems and appropriate facilitation will keep students engaged in the problem and focused on its outcome. Remember that problem design and facilitation are the keys here. Using PBL does require careful preparation and active coaching. The small groups allow for more even participation by students than the typical large-group classroom setting. When students are active participants in the direction and outcome of their learning and are genuinely busy, they have little time or cause to be disruptive or "off task."

- Teachers should bear in mind that PBL offers opportunities for cognitive, psychological, and emotional development in ways that many traditional approaches do not. However, PBL is not an answer to all educational issues. As questions arise about what to do when using PBL if certain controversial issues do present themselves, teachers are reminded to consider what they are currently doing to manage those issues. Often, the strategies that are already in place will work very well alongside PBL instruction.

•◆6▲■

Putting PBL to
Work and to the Test

*I should have liked to be asked to say what I knew. They
always tried to ask what I did not know. When I would will-
ingly have displayed my knowledge, they sought to expose
my ignorance. This sort of treatment had only one result: I
did not do well in examinations.*

—Winston Churchill (1874-1965)

Integrating PBL With the
Curriculum: Three Suggestions

A number of PBL problem scenarios have been provided in the
preceding chapters. These should be used as templates for creating your own problems. When you begin to write a PBL scenario
using these models, be certain to adhere consistently to the qualities that define effective PBL scenarios.

- First, identify the students' role early in the problem. This gives them the reason to want to know the needed information. Notice in the examples that each problem begins with "You are . . . ." Remember to put the students in roles that are relevant to their world, the interests they have, and their capacity for understanding the role.

As you develop the scenarios, guard against overwhelming students with too much information. Inexperienced scenario writers tend to fear that students will not pursue the intended content areas unless they are directed to do so by the problem scenario. The common mistake is to overload the problem with too many facts and too much detail. It is more important to provide the students with a rich story line that will prompt their curiosity about the intended content objectives.

- Second, novice writers must also be careful not to create task statements disguised as PBL problems. Even veteran PBL teachers occasionally fall into this trap, often when they are in a hurry to prepare a problem. An example of a task statement disguised as a PBL problem is "You are in the third grade in Mrs. Hudson's class. She has just explained that you will soon be studying about Japan and need to understand the culture there." A more genuine PBL scenario to prompt the same content objectives would be "Our class has the opportunity to have a Japanese pen pal. Here is what we know about her so far. She is your age and in the same grade. She will be visiting the United States in 6 months. She is curious to know something about the differences between her daily life and yours." Students will need to know about her daily life to compare it with their own. The students will figure this out and be interested in doing the research. The PBL scenario is student directed, whereas the task statement is teacher directed.
- The third suggestion is that once you have developed a PBL problem, read it aloud or preview it with at least one other person before introducing it to your class. This will help you predict how the problem will be interpreted by someone other than yourself. Ask your previewer to tell you what he or she thinks

children will say they need to know and what he or she thinks the intended objectives are. Sometimes teachers know what they intend for a problem to do, but they may not have translated that effectively into the problem. This quick preview often reveals if the problem needs to be revised or just tweaked before being introducing to students.

Finding PBL Problem Scenarios: Local and National Standards

Remember that sources for PBL scenarios are all around you. A defining characteristic of PBL problem scenarios is that they show up in the student's real world, so use that real world as a problem source. Newspaper articles, school issues, and family or social issues are relevant to students and are usually ripe with concepts that match most courses of study and local, state, or national objectives.

- Use your own standard course of study or state/national objectives as a blueprint for problem development. Identify and make a list of the objectives that you would like students to understand before you write the problem scenario. Next, create a story line that will appeal to your learners and quickly interest them in pursuing the learning objectives you have outlined. For example, *The National Science Education Standards* (National Research Council, 1996) identifies content standards at all grade levels. One of the content standards in the area of life science indicates that all K-4 students should "develop an understanding of: the characteristics of organisms, the life cycles of organisms, and organisms and environments" (p. 106).

With these objectives in mind, PBL teachers developed some of the example cases for kindergarten and first-grade students provided in Chapter 2. *We'll Take Care of It* prompts the children to consider animals appropriate for a classroom pet and the type of environment needed to support such a pet. *Where's the Great Pumpkin?* encourages the students to explore why vegetables failed to grow or rotted after growth. In Chapter 3, for students in Grades 2-3, *Creepy, Crawly Caterpillars* has the children explore the value of different organisms to their environment. The objectives for these problems were derived from national standards and were then easily aligned with local standards.

- Other teachers begin with local standards to identify the objectives for a PBL problem scenario. An example of this strategy is in the problem *Samuel, Sarah, and You* found in Chapter 3 for second and third graders. The state (in this case, North Carolina) defines the social studies curriculum and includes specific goals and objectives. One of the goals is: "The learner will infer that individuals, families, and communities are and have been alike and different." Within that broad goal the specific objectives are:

  > Distinguish similarities and differences among children at different times and in different places; analyze similarities and differences among families in different times and in different places; and assess similarities and differences among communities in different times and in different places.

All of these objectives are effectively included in the PBL problem *Samuel, Sarah, and You.*

Another example of using local standards is in the problem *Patty O'Design* found in Chapter 4 for Grades 4-6. This problem aligns with state competencies for mathematics. The major concept included in this problem is the understanding of points, lines, angles, and transformations in geometry. The specific North Carolina state objectives found in this problem are:

> Identify points, lines, and angles in the environment; use manipulatives, pictorial representations, and appropriate vocabulary to identify the properties of plane figures in the environment; measure the perimeter of rectangles and triangles; determine the area of rectangles and squares using grids; and find areas of other regular and irregular figures using grids.

Again, each of these objectives is embedded in the problem as the students design a patio specific to the criteria they are given by

their "clients." Multiple solutions are possible, but the viable solutions require the students to explore and understand the intended objectives.

- Once teachers become comfortable with PBL, they often opt to
  use PBL units to meet the curriculum goals. PBL units typically
  consist of three or four PBL cases that have been developed to
  use over a longer period of time and to include more objectives.
  One PBL unit for third-grade students is called The Garden
  Unit. It consists of three PBL problem cases: *Where Does Your
  Garden Grow?*, *What Does Your Garden Grow?*, and *How Does
  Your Garden Grow?* The emphasis of this unit is on science competency goals as defined by North Carolina for third graders.
  The goals are for the learner to build an understanding of plant
  growth, plant adaptations, and soil concepts. The students are
  put into a variety of roles over a 4- to 6-week period as they
  progress through the different PBL problems. This maintains
  their interest and provides ample opportunities to include many
  specific objectives that fall within this competency.

The children are agricultural extension agents in one problem, and that role leads them to do soil testing and investigate
ways to improve the soil for crop production. In another problem, the children are given the role of landscape architects and
must design an aesthetically pleasing garden, working within a
limited budget, that can be supported by the soil conditions. In
the third problem, the children are science teachers attempting
to find the best location for a class garden. These three PBL
problem scenarios effectively address the specific goals of the
science competencies mentioned above. In all, there are 19 specific goals embedded in this one PBL unit. Teachers often report,
however, that students exceed those goals by including additional areas on their Learning Issues lists. Budgeting is embedded
in one problem and is a math competency. Measuring for garden
design is a component of two of the problems and is also a math
competency. As agricultural extension agents, students must
develop a plan of action for improving soil, and they must
communicate this to the client. Writing and oral communication
competencies are thus also addressed.

Teachers are encouraged to capture not only the intended objectives of PBL problems but also those that students identify. Any other objectives that come up from another component of the overall curriculum should also be documented. Doing so develops a comprehensive record of all the objectives addressed while engaging PBL problems. From this record, teachers can easily develop a PBL blueprint to reference in lesson planning that will help to integrate PBL at strategic points for any subject area in the comprehensive curriculum.

Making the PBL Grade: Authentic Assessments

It is important to keep in mind that assessing the student learning that occurs during PBL instruction is likely to be quite different from traditional assessment strategies. Just as teachers are sometimes initially uncomfortable with PBL instruction, the same is true when it comes to assessing students in a manner consistent with PBL instruction. To assist in distinguishing traditional assessment methods from those that support PBL instruction, the term *authentic assessments* will be used to describe PBL assessment.

Authentic assessments have distinguishing features that both characterize them and align them with PBL instruction. Those features include collecting evidence from multiple activities, measuring student learning by engaging them in examples of what you want students to be able to do, and continuing to promote learning throughout the assessment process.

Traditional assessments are typically an audit of performance. They often measure what students can recall on a certain day. These assessments rarely have a component that leads to improved performance. Rather, they simply measure and report ability to recall and do not include a process for addressing knowledge gaps or providing deeper feedback to the student. This is because traditional assessments also tend to focus on uncovering what students do not know. Although it is important to target knowledge gaps that students may have, it is too often the case that these gaps are exposed and then left unattended. Students typically receive a graded quiz or exam with the wrong answers marked but no follow-up explanation for why answers are incorrect or further instruction to correct or deepen understanding. Additionally, traditional assessments often disrupt learning. Students will stop the learning process to memorize information or cram facts and details in order to perform well on traditional short-term recall examinations.

In contrast, the authentic assessments used to support PBL instruction often occur throughout the learning process, with perhaps a culminating activity or demonstration of student achievement, such as an oral or written report, poster, or constructed model, at the end of the problem. Such assessments are designed to give the student specific feedback about his or her understanding and to improve the student's performance. Authentic assessments reveal and emphasize the understanding that has occurred and allow opportunities to correct areas of misunderstanding or oversight.

Authentic assessments are also designed to support evaluating the critical reasoning process as well as the content acquisition of students. Effective PBL assessments evaluate the student's performance as a group member. The quality of work within each of these areas—content acquisition, reasoning and thinking process, and collaborating for effective outcomes—is considered for its value to the student's growth and the group's performance.

Working from these examples may help in understanding effective ways to structure the assessment plan you use in conjunction with PBL.

PBL and Assessment Examples

Content assessment in PBL is designed to demonstrate the students' understanding of concepts and their ability to apply that understanding. Feedback on the quality of content acquisition should be given throughout the duration of the PBL problem. The teacher provides this feedback as groups are monitored during the PBL process. This may be done by asking prompting questions, commenting on what students have researched, or having the students self-assess their progress. This allows students to improve their performance during content acquisition and, ideally, to deepen their understanding.

- An example of a content assessment rubric is given below. This simple rubric accompanies the PBL problem *Moonball*, which is described in Chapter 5. Remember, in this problem, students are to suggest changes in the existing rules and regulations for the way basketball is played on Earth to the way it would be played on the moon. They are then asked to expand the newly formed Moon Basketball Association to an interplanetary league by making further suggestions to adapt the rules and regulations.

Score	Criteria
5	Three changes in the rules and regulations CLEARLY explained for more than three celestial bodies. Accurately completed worksheet.
4	Three changes in the rules and regulations CLEARLY explained for at least two celestial bodies. Accurately completed worksheet.
3	Three changes in the rules and regulations CLEARLY explained for at least the moon. Accurately completed worksheet.
2	At least one change in the rules and regulations CLEARLY explained for the moon.
1	At least one change in the rules and regulations has been proposed. It does not have a clear scientific explanation.
0	No changes in the rules and regulations explained.

In this example, students must demonstrate an understanding of the concepts around gravitational forces. A worksheet on calculating weight changes for Earth, Pluto, Jupiter, Saturn, and the moon is provided with the problem. Students receive no credit for proposing changes in the rules and regulations that they cannot scientifically explain. Each group presents their proposed changes to the class or in a written format to the teacher. It is encouraged to have students report orally when time allows, even if a written report is also provided. This gives students the chance to practice oral presentation and to demonstrate their ability to explain what they have learned. The teacher determines the achieved score and gives that to each group member.

Only content acquisition has been assessed in this example. In PBL, it is equally important to assess the process used for arriving at solutions to the problem. This component is what helps to ensure that students can transfer the process from one problem to another, enhancing their ability to apply what they learn to different situations. Because the PBL process is interdependent rather than independent, it is practical to assess the students' collaboration skills as part of their skill with the process. On the next page is an example of a longer rubric used to assess an individual student's group and process skills.

A similar rubric has criteria that are slightly more sophisticated in regard to the PBL process. This rubric may become more appropriate as students gain experience with the method, or with older students.

The teacher rates the students on the categories given (or similar ones of his or her own choosing) as the students work through the PBL problem. Teachers are encouraged to give students feedback on the quality of their contributions in these categories as work progresses, thus giving them time to improve any areas of weakness. It is suggested that teachers make notes about individual student performances that heavily influence the overall rating. For example, if a student asks good-quality, probing questions that move the group toward better understanding, that behavior should be noted for the student. On the other hand, if a student constantly throws out nonsensical questions just to be part of the conversation and derails the process, that behavior should also be noted for the student.

These observations should be shared with the student at an appropriate time along with suggestions for improving areas of weakness. Where these observations concern areas of strength, students should be encouraged to help other students strengthen their performances in similar ways. The overall rating should be

Individual Student Assessment in Group

Student Name: _____ Problem Case: _____

Rate each individual's performance as:
4 = Excellent
3 = Good
2 = Fair
1 = Poor
0 = Unscorable

	Student Names							
Date								
Criteria								
Participates in groupwork								
Contributes to project success								
Listens to others								
Asks and answers questions								
Stays on task								
Finds and contributes quality information								
Cooperates with others								
Offers positive suggestions								
Exhibits leadership								
Compliments and encourages others								
Overall rating								

Individual Student Assessment in Group

Student Name: _____ Problem Case: _____

Rate each individual's performance as:
4 = Excellent
3 = Good
2 = Fair
1 = Poor
0 = Unscorable

	Student Names							
Date								
Criteria								
Generates effective learning issues								
Demonstrates hypothesis proposal and testing								
Grasps new concepts								
Applies new information								
Shows skill at teaching peers								
Demonstrates cooperation and consensus building								
Participates effectively in group process								
Identifies and shares appropriate resources								
Demonstrates growth of knowledge								
Exhibits functional, decisive, and focused qualities								
Exhibits leadership appropriately								
Encourages others with useful feedback								

determined when the PBL problem is completed. Each student receives an individual rating on the group/process performance component of assessment.

- Another element of authentic assessment is in weighting the components of content acquisition, individual contribution to group process, and collaboration skills. The weight assigned to each area carries a message to the students about where to concentrate their energies and efforts. Let's say, for example, that the content assessment is to contribute to a student's overall grade for the quarter or semester in a subject area the same as a quiz score would, maybe 10%, but the individual group process score is weighted at 5%. The teacher could, of course, weight these differently in different assignments. However, with this kind of distribution, the message to students is that knowing the content is more important than contributing effectively to the group process. Students may be less concerned with sharing resources or encouraging others than they are with showing that they have learned new material. However, both are important when assessing PBL activities.

Teachers are cautioned to weight the assessments appropriately to support the PBL methodology. Another caution is to limit the assessment topic areas to three or four major categories, or else the teacher will become an accountant.

- For lengthy PBL problems, the use of a portfolio is recommended. In this design, students can demonstrate their content acquisition and their skill at critical thinking in a variety of formats. For example, a portfolio may contain a learning log in which students list their Need to Know items or Learning Issues and then describe the resources used to research those. Evidence of the research, such as a report or worksheet, becomes part of the portfolio. On the following page is an example of a learning log for the problem *Red Eye to Pluto* (found in Appendix B).

Students receive the log as an empty grid. They complete the grid cells as they progress through the PBL problem. The column for evidence identifies the material that they will include in their

Student Learning Log

Student Name: _____   Problem Case: _Red Eye to Pluto_

Date	Learning Issue	Resource(s)	Evidence
3-13	How far is each planet from Earth?	Science books, Internet, encyclopedia	Diagram of the solar system
3-13	How far is each planet from each other?	Science books, Internet, encyclopedia	Diagram of the solar system
3-13	What does each planet look like?	Science books, Internet, encyclopedia, books on solar system	Picture and written description of each planet
3-14	What equation calculates the amount of the fare?	Math textbook	Worksheet showing fares for each planet
3-14	How do you plan routes to make the most profit?	Worksheet with fares	Diagram with cost of each possible fare

portfolio to demonstrate they have researched and understood the learning issue. Notice that, at times, their evidence for one learning issue may serve as a resource for a different learning issue. This use of their own evidence reinforces the students' understanding of the material and their ability to apply that understanding to problem resolutions.

The portfolio often contains a writing component that is persuasive and that requires the students to defend their most viable solution. Students may support their defense by including newspaper articles, Web site references, or collected pamphlets and brochures. They may draw diagrams or pictures to demonstrate why one solution is desirable over another. The teacher determines the criteria for the writing component, such as a business letter format, short report, or essay.

A distinct advantage of a portfolio is that it allows for assessment to occur throughout the problem in a documented form. Students may turn in the portfolio at various stages of completion and receive formative feedback. They may then have a chance to revise the earlier work in order to improve their performance, and they will have specific guidelines for the remainder of the work to be completed.

- Examples of other authentic assessments include observations of student performance, work samples, and projects. It is most effective to provide the students with a copy of the scoring form or checklist to be used for assessment when the assignment is made. The teacher should provide the criteria to be assessed; they should be distinctly outlined, and whenever possible, they should include a model or example to be followed. Students should also understand how gradations in quality will be assessed from not acceptable to exemplary and any categories in between.

In determining your assessment plan to support PBL instruction, it is helpful to remember that one of the PBL characteristics is the problem's relation to the real world. Consider how assessment occurs in the real world and incorporate similar elements into your plan. This will help your students become familiar, comfortable, and skillful at being assessed in performance situations.

PBL and the Future

Educators and education experts have explored many trends in attempts to improve student performance, improve teacher practices, and graduate students who are well prepared for higher education or the job market. So many trends have been explored, it seems, that teachers often refer to them as "the flavor of the month." Sustainability of such trends is often not evident, and teachers typically return to their own comfortable style once they have tried out a new practice. This appears not to be the case with PBL teachers and for good reasons.

Teachers report that in addition to the many student benefits of PBL, there are numerous teacher benefits. PBL teachers experience the fundamental elements of teaching that first attracted them to the profession. They interact more with their students; they share the joy of discovery with their students; they share the pride of accomplishment with their students. Teachers say they feel they are making a greater impact on students' lives by giving them the skills to learn on their own. Most teachers came to the profession hoping to influence and affect their students' lives in meaningful ways. They feel that PBL provides more and better chances to do this. And at the end of the day, teachers say it is both more fun and more effective to teach and learn using PBL.

This helps explain the sustainability of PBL, and that explains why its use is becoming more widespread. Although medical schools are credited with being the birthplace of PBL, its prevalence has spread to other professional graduate schools, 4-year universities, community colleges, and many K-12 school systems.

Today, all 125 medical schools in the United States report at least a PBL component within their curriculum. Others report a full transition to a PBL course of study. Likewise, most veterinary schools report the use of PBL throughout the curriculum. At Samford University in Birmingham, Alabama, the Center for Problem-Based Learning recently developed a list of undergraduate institutions that shows that 74 universities self-report that they offer PBL courses. Of those 74, at least 16 have extensive outreach programs to K-12 school systems. It is likely that this number underrepresents the current level of activity in PBL initiatives. Whatever the true number currently is, the evidence is clear that the practice of PBL continues to grow and is being sustained.

Community colleges have demonstrated a significant increase in the use of PBL over the past 10 years as the result of a major initiative, the Curriculum Improvement Project. In North Carolina alone, a recent PBL Conference for Community College Faculty attracted 93 participants, representing 70% of the community colleges in the state system.

The use of PBL has grown well beyond the standard of "a trend." Rather, PBL, as a methodology to address many educational concerns and criticisms, is becoming a prevalent practice. For instance, Southern Illinois University School of Medicine has reported rapid dissemination of the methodology within School District 186 in Springfield, Illinois. It was further reported that teachers there perceive PBL as the solution to many problems in K-12 education.

PBL addresses many concerns one sees daily in the media as well as professional journals. Problems include uninterested students, poor scores on standardized national examinations, low retention of learned material, inability to apply previously learned information, and low evidence of critical and higher-order thinking skills. In the information-driven and technology-oriented society we have today and will have in the future, there is significant concern over these issues. PBL addresses these deficiencies and does so in the absence of rote, mundane, "skill and drill" exercises. Instead, PBL gives meaning to the learning that takes place. It gives relevancy to the information, which supports retention and transferability to different situations. Additionally, as more and more postsecondary institutions incorporate PBL practices, students' successful preparation must begin during their K-12 experiences. For students who move directly into employment after high school graduation, the advantages from PBL experiences will serve them much better in the world of work.

The good news is that the use of PBL does not require classroom teachers to abandon the strategies and approaches that have worked well for them. PBL gives these practices a context that makes them more meaningful and more effective. Teachers have already acknowledged the value of collaborative learning, problem-solving exercises, and independent study. PBL provides a framework that integrates these successful strategies and, at the same time, puts excitement back into learning.

This book is not meant to give the impression that PBL can and will fix all the ills in the current educational system. It is intended, however, that teachers find here a useful and meaningful strategy to increase student learning that complements many of the things they are already successfully doing. The hope is that teachers will find as many benefits for themselves as for their students. Teachers have always been the source of the dedication, inspiration, and enthusiasm that create the kind of momentum necessary to make meaningful changes in classroom practices. The true merit of this book is, perhaps, in providing the spark that feeds the passion and perseverance of classroom teachers.

Educators should hold a vision for the future that includes preparing students in the best possible ways for postsecondary experiences, whether in higher education or work. That foundation, in order to meet the demands of today's and tomorrow's society, will prepare students with an extensive, integrated knowledge base that is effectively retained and easily recalled. It will give students the necessary skills to acquire information on their own and apply it in problem-solving situations. Students will be prepared to be effective collaborators with peers and supervisors. And, perhaps most important, students will have developed the self-directed learning skills to be effective, independent learners for the rest of their lives.

● Appendix A ■

PBL Facilitator Do's and Don'ts: Suggestions for Prompting and Guiding Students

Facilitator Do's

- Do use open-ended prompting questions, such as:
    What would it be helpful to know now?
    Is that a learning issue?
    How do you know that?
    What does that have to do with the problem?
    Does everyone agree with that statement?
    Where are you stuck?
    Can you agree on what the next step should be?
    Say more about what you are thinking about that.
    Where can you find that kind of information?
    Somebody summarize where you are right now.
    What do you agree to do before you meet about this again?
- Do make brief notes to yourself before intervening.
- Do count to 10 or 20 before intervening.
- Do give students time to self-correct before you do it for them.

- Do be in the problem with the students rather than being an observer who knows how it turns out.
- Do be patient and let the students make mistakes. Powerful learning occurs in mistake making.
- Do help students discover how to correct mistakes and avoid the same ones in the future.
- Do get excited with the students and enjoy the learning with them.

Facilitator Don'ts

- Don't take the problem away from the students by being too directive.
- Don't send messages that they are thinking the "wrong" way or doing the "wrong" thing.
- Don't give them too much information because you are afraid they won't find it.
- Don't intervene the moment you sense they are off track—remember, mistakes are okay.
- Don't rush them, especially in the beginning.
- Don't be afraid to say, "That sounds like a learning issue to me," instead of telling them the "answer."
- Don't worry. Students will learn lots of content, become sound critical thinkers, and enjoy PBL lesson days.

● Appendix B ■

Additional PBL Problem
Examples by Grade Level

Additional PBL problem examples by grade level are provided in this section.

Grades K-1

Grasshoppers Galore!!

You live on a farm in nearby Cedar Grove. Your neighbor has had an infestation of grasshoppers. According to a newspaper article that was written about your neighbor's problem, there are so many grasshoppers that even the experts are shocked. This does not normally happen in this area.

What can the farmer do about all these grasshoppers?

The children are guided to consider things such as:

Where did all these grasshoppers come from?
How can you tell a grasshopper from other insects?

Why did they come to the neighbor's farm and not theirs?
Do grasshoppers do good things to the places they live?
Do grasshoppers do bad things to the places they live?
What are safe ways to get rid of grasshoppers?

This problem contains math, science, and communication skills as intended objectives. Teachers have a lot of room in this problem to steer children to the science goals about identifying insects, insect life cycles, and insect and environment interactions. If the teacher chooses to have students pursue the math goals, she may have to be more directive to get students to consider measuring the area of the farm, calculating the area of the invasion, and measuring in different units. The communication skill objectives may be embedded in how the children convey the information they gather about the problem to the neighbor and the community. They might write a newspaper article themselves, because one is referenced in the original scenario.

Teddy Bear Hugs

Our classroom is in charge of a special project. There are many people at our school who help take care of us and keep us safe. Our project is to choose one of these people and let him or her know that this care and concern is appreciated. We have a limited budget to work with on this project.

Who are the people we should consider?
What kinds of things show that someone is appreciated?

This problem has objectives in character education, math, and communication skills.

Teachers typically make this a true "real-world" PBL by having the children identify whom they would like to acknowledge from their list of people. The students then determine what they can do to show their appreciation. They usually suggest baking a cake, making a card, planting a flower, or making a painting. The teacher then has each group actually make their acknowledgment item and plan a way to present the gift to the chosen person.

Tweet, Tweet, Let's Eat

Today you and some of your friends noticed that there are birds around the school yard. You all remember that birds usually go south for winter, and it is already December. Back in your classroom, the teacher explains that the birds are probably still here because the fall weather was so warm that some of the birds did not migrate. Now, she asks the class, "What can we do to help the birds that stayed here survive the cold weather and find enough food to eat?"

What do birds usually eat?
Why is that a problem during cold weather?
How do birds usually stay warm?
Why is that a problem now?

The objectives for this problem are science related and include making observations, caring for living organisms, and interacting with the environment.

Some teachers have also made this a true "real-world" problem by having the children design and build bird feeders. The bird feeders are then placed near the classroom where the children can observe how often the feeders are visited. Birdhouses have also been constructed, models of nests have been made, and birdseed has been placed in sheltered areas.

Grades 2-3

Rock and Roll

My dad says that I use rocks in my mouth, but I think he is just kidding. My mom says that my clothes have a rocky-fresh smell. I think she is off her rocker. My teacher says my parents are correct, that I use rocks every day without even knowing it. To prove it, we have to work in small groups and create a rock museum, highlighting the products we get from rocks.

What do you think your Dad meant about rocks in your mouth?
Why did your Mom say your clothes smell like rocks?
What other things do we use that come from rocks?

The intended objectives include analyzing and evaluating rock composition, learning how to gather and display information, relating new information to personal experiences, and making predictions. The teacher may provide rock samples or reference books to assist the children in identifying different types of rocks. She might also bring in various products or have the children bring these in to match a variety of rocks. A rock quarry is a good resource and, perhaps, a field trip experience.

Edonton Pond

You are a member of the County Planning Board. You have been asked to plan a community around a nearby pond. Different members of the area approach you to be sure that you include certain things in the plan. Your team is responsible for designing a plan to present a model of what the area around the pond would look like. You must consider how your plan will affect the plants and animals that live in the area now.

What is a County Planning Board?

What makes up a community?

What kinds of things in a community affect plants and animals?

This problem is typically used after the students have already learned a significant amount of content information about the interdependence of plants and animals, adaptation of animals, and preservation of the environment. This problem gives the students the opportunity to use that information in context and to demonstrate their depth of understanding as they create and defend their designs.

Light, Color, and Where Do Rainbows Come From?

Scenario 1: It has just stopped raining. You look out the window and notice the drops of rain as they fall from leaves on the tree. The sun has just begun to peek from behind the last gray clouds that were in the sky. You grab your favorite ball and open the front door. The air is still moist, and THERE IT IS! The rainbow! The colors are soft pastels. They arch across the sky, fading gently behind the houses at the other end of the neighborhood. You begin to wonder . . .

What makes a rainbow?

How do colors get to be in the sky?

Scenario 2: You begin to play ball in the driveway. You notice an oil spot where a car has been parked, and there it is again, another rainbow. This one is different, though.

What caused the rainbow in the driveway?

How is it different from the rainbow in the sky?

Scenario 3: After you get tired of playing ball, you decide to blow bubbles. You get your bubbles and take them outside. As the bubbles you blow rise up toward the sky and in the direction of the sun, there is ANOTHER RAINBOW. It looks like it is in the bubbles.

What caused the rainbow in the bubbles?

Are the colors the same as the other rainbows you have seen?

What is the same about all three rainbows?

The objectives for this problem include understanding pigment, reflection, refraction, and how light travels. There are a number of classroom activities for making rainbows. Teachers may already be aware of these, or they may find them in science textbooks and on the Internet. Other activities, such as producing color change and chromatography experiments, are also a good complement to this problem.

Swings 'n' Things

Our school is building a new playground. Our class has been asked to submit a proposal or model of the ideal playground to the principal. The PTA fund-raiser this year will give $15,000 to build the playground.

What would you like to see on the new playground?

How can we be sure we make a safe playground?

What else would be helpful to know about a new playground?

Usually, students will need to know where the playground will be located, how large it will be, and what playground equipment costs. The teacher should be prepared to provide this information to the students. The location and size of the playground is flexible depending on the school. Playground equipment catalogs or Internet sites give the students an idea of the expenses involved.

This problem has math, safety, and communication objectives. Some teachers take the children to a site on the school grounds to measure the dimensions they are given. Children may actually graph the area to determine the amount of room needed to safely install different pieces of playground equipment. Most teachers have each group write a proposal for their design. The proposal should be persuasive and should include the budget for the proposed design.

Grades 4-5

Eekosisstim

As an up-and-coming young producer/director, you have been asked by a major studio to create a story about a small ecosystem being destroyed by humanoid pollutants. It will need insectlike characters, a threatened habitat, and a plot/story line that would appeal to a young audience. You have an unlimited budget and artistic freedom to decide how the story will be presented. The studio board has requested that you submit your initial proposal in 30 days.

What additional information do you need to proceed?

How will this information help you to begin your plan to produce this story?

What are your initial thoughts about how to proceed?

The main learning objective is for the students to develop an understanding of the interdependence of plants and animals. Additional learning areas include understanding how television programs and movies are developed and produced. Students are likely to explore a variety of insects to determine their story characters' characteristics. They may decide to explore set design or different film techniques. The teacher can determine how long this problem will continue and if she is comfortable with the students' choosing learning areas outside of the intended objectives. Often, the students remain engaged in an ongoing problem as long as they can pursue the additional learning areas that they choose. The teacher will need to ensure that the students are balancing their time appropriately to explore both the intended objectives and the additional areas of interest.

Red Eye to Pluto

You have recently gotten a job with the Ford Prefect Red Eye to Pluto taxi service. Your job requires that you drive your space taxi from planet to planet transporting passengers. The planets all differ greatly in distance from Earth and in size, too. After completing a trip, you return to planet Earth to refuel and get your next dispatch. Your boss is waiting and gives you this extra assignment: "I want you to calculate the cost of your next 10 trips to see if our fares need to be adjusted."

What do you already know about how far the planets are from Earth?

What would it be helpful to know to calculate the fares?

Will the size of the planets affect the cost of the taxi ride? Why or why not?

The learning areas for this problem may include a wide range of solar system issues, communication, computation, budgeting, and an understanding of the profit/loss concept.

This problem has its own set of references, called "Fact Sheets," to provide some of the information that the students will need but will not be able to locate on their own. One Fact Sheet contains the company's fare for travel to a planet and additional fare to orbit the planet. The fares vary depending on the distance from Earth and the size of the planet. Another Fact Sheet contains the distances of each planet from Earth. Although students can locate this information using a variety of sources, some teachers prefer to have the comprehensive list available once the students indicate they need this information. Teachers should feel free to develop resources such as Fact Sheets that they feel help in the flow of the problem. Bookmarking good Internet resources is another way to provide needed facts to the students.

Additional scenarios are provided with this problem to assist the students in calculating and projecting the costs of their taxi-cab trips. Samples of two of those scenarios follow.

Scenario 2: At the departure gate on Earth, a large Inki, who doesn't speak your language, holds up a card that looks like this: [A CARD WITH THE PICTURE OF ANY PLANET]. Upon your arrival at the Inki's destination, the space traffic controller tells you to orbit the planet twice because of fog. You are finally able to deliver the Inki and head back to Earth.

Scenario 3: You get a call to pick up a Walrussian at the space-port on Earth and take her to her home-base station on Neptune. Because of the traffic at the spaceport, you are ordered to orbit the planet once.

For both scenarios, children must calculate the distance required to orbit each planet (which differs depending on the planet's size) and then adjust the fare accordingly. This should be understood from the original task in the problem, but teachers are there to facilitate its happening.

This problem could be used to introduce or to wrap up a unit on the solar system or computation skills. It could be used with both subject areas simultaneously. This type of problem can be expanded to occur over several weeks by including multiple scenarios and emphasizing multiple learning areas. Similarly, the problem can be shortened by directing the students to fewer learning areas and by providing fewer scenarios.

Foreign Exchange

Your best friend's family recently moved to _____ [fill this in with the country of focus for the problem]. You have been invited to spend some of your vacation time with them. Although the family has made some plans for your visit, they have also asked you to make suggestions about things you would like to do during your 2-week visit. You also need to find out what things you need to do in order to travel to a foreign country.

What do you already know about _____?
What do you think would be helpful to know?

The intended learning objectives for this problem include understanding that individuals, families, and communities are different; understanding the existence of a variety of cultural traditions; and communication skills. Additional objectives may come up in this problem about time zones, geographical regions, transportation options, and travel costs. Teachers sometimes assign a different country or region to four or five different groups. Each group then presents the ideas they have about travel to that country using a poster, brochure, or postcards that they create.

Don't Turn Off the Light

You are the governor's adviser on the preservation of historic sites. He needs your advice about whether to move the Hatteras Lighthouse or to explore ways to protect it where it sits. He has asked you to prepare a proposal supporting one of these two options.

Why do you think it would be necessary to move or protect a lighthouse?

What are things you would need to consider in moving a lighthouse?

What are things you would need to consider in leaving the lighthouse where it is?

This is an example of a problem taken from current events in the students' home state. In 1997, there was significant debate in North Carolina over the merits of moving the lighthouse at Cape Hatteras versus putting protective mechanisms along the coastal area to ensure its safety. The students studied beach erosion, made predictions about future erosion, and considered the history of the lighthouse, its status as a state symbol, and the expenses involved in each option. The students were able to follow the statewide debate through newspaper articles and television reports. They eventually were able to watch a news telecast as the lighthouse was actually moved to a safer place.

The problem is still used even though the original dilemma has been addressed. Students study mostly the same areas and make predictions about the future of the lighthouse in its current location.

Grades 6-8

A Thought for Your Penny

You work in research and development at the U.S. Mint. You are assigned to design a new penny for the future. It must be tarnishproof and maintain the same size and mass as a standard penny.

What do you already know about the size and mass of pennies?

Are there rules or regulations about what can be put on the design of a coin?

What makes something tarnishproof?

The objectives for this problem include mass, weight, properties of metals, alloys, design, cost of metals, and communication skills. There are many effective existing labs on matter that teachers should feel free to bring into this problem. Flame testing and electroplating activities are two suggestions. Another suggestion, to effectively embed the communication objectives, is to have the students write a letter to the U.S. Mint that includes their new penny design and explains its merits.

Let's Go to the Fair

You are a design engineer at Fun Time Designs. Mr. Newton, president and owner of the Fair Days Amusement Park, is in need of some engineering expertise to restore the park. He wishes to restore the original Newtonian Adventure Themes section of the park. (Mr. Newton is the descendant of a very famous scientist, and he would like the park to reflect as many of his ancestor's discoveries as possible.) Some of the rides are in excellent shape, but others need repair and replacement. Mr. Newton's immediate concern is to get new designs to replace the rides that are not operational and not repairable.

The first ride that Mr. Newton wants to build is the vertical fall ride. This ride must meet the following criteria:

1. The actual ride should include a fall of between 8.0 and 10.0 meters.

2. Figures for acceleration at ground zero should be calculated.

The design of all rides should include mechanical drawings, should be tested and retested, and should meet all safety requirements before being built and open to the public. Scale models and demonstrations of each ride are required.

Who is Mr. Newton's ancestor?
What kinds of discoveries did he make?
How will this affect your designs for rides in the park?

This problem has multiple scenarios to keep the students engaged in the intended learning areas.

Scenario 2: Because of Fun Time Designs' success with the vertical fall ride, Mr. Newton has asked that you design a ride that: (a) is not powered by gravity or a motor, (b) needs to accelerate from a resting position, (c) is not limited to ground travel, and (d) must travel horizontally for a period of time. The model to be demonstrated to Mr. Newton should be able to travel a minimum of 1.5 meters and a maximum of 3.0 meters and remain within a width of 1.0 meter.

Scenario 3: Mr. Newton has now asked Fun Time Designs to create a third ride for his amusement park completely different from the other two rides. This ride is (a) to be powered by gravity, (b) to be self-stopping, and (c) to be able to travel horizontally part of the time. The model of the ride should run at least 4.0 meters and no more than 5.0 meters in length, and remain within a width of 1.0 meter.

The use of all three scenarios comprises an eighth-grade physics unit. This unit typically lasts for about 3 weeks. The learning objectives include understanding gravitational forces, friction and motion relationships, Newton's laws, measurement, indirect proportion, and simple machines.

Amphibian Anxiety

Mr. Jack Dewey, director of Camp Malf, received a letter from a concerned parent whose child came home from camp and described deformed frogs in the area where camp activities were taking place. The parent wants to know if frogs in the area are indeed deformed, and, if so, if the children are at any risk. You are on the consultant team Mr. Dewey has hired to advise him on an appropriate response. Mr. Dewey wants you to study the frog deformation problem and determine if there is a potential hazard to the campers. You may wish to gather data as well as interpret data collected by other scientists. You will be reporting your findings regularly.

What do you think the parent means by "deformed"?
What else would it be helpful to know to start your investigation?

This problem comes with a map of the area that shows a lake and the adjoining camp property. The map shows the location of other nearby properties such as an abandoned air base, a housing development, a Christmas tree farm, and agricultural land growing apples and tobacco. The primary learning objective is to develop an understanding of human and environmental interaction. Students typically research factors in the development of amphibians as well.

● Appendix C ■

Completed PBL Process Chart, Single Chart

Case Name: *Weather Watch*

Fact List	Need to Know	Learning Issues
You are home alone with your baby-sitter. Your Mom and Dad are still at work. A warning on TV says there might be a flood because of a storm.	What time is it? Is it dark outside? When will parents be home? Can baby-sitter drive? Are adult neighbors home?	How long must it storm before it floods? Why do some places flood and not others? How do weather forecasters know ahead of time that a storm is coming? How do weather forecasters know a flood will develop from rainfall in a storm?

Possible Solutions	New Learning Issues
Call parents for advice. Keep watching TV for more news. Go stay with a neighbor. Go someplace higher than where we are if the storm really comes.	Do we have an upstairs in the house? What is high enough up if a flood starts to develop? How long does it take floodwater to go away?

Defendable Solution(s)
A safe plan showing where to go or what to do during severe weather conditions, especially when parents are not at home.
A safe plan for when parents are at home.

This or a similar form is the basic document in the PBL process. It may be structured slightly differently, or it may take two to three pages, but the categories are constant.

● Appendix D ■

Completed PBL Process Chart, Multiple Charts

Case Name: *Player's Choice, Day 1*

Fact List	Need to Know	Learning Issues
Statistician for NBA team Analyze data for 15 players Select five best for starting lineup Make graphic presentation	Statistics on the players: field goals, free throws, steals, turnovers, assists, rebounds, personal fouls, blocks, minutes played	What are averages? How are statistics compiled, and who does it? How do you know what statistics represent? How do you make a graphic presentation of information? What is percent/ratio in statistics?

Possible Solutions	New Learning Issues
Any lineup with five players with stats that can be defended. A lineup with five players who have highest field goals, assisting, and high playing time. A lineup with five players who have high scoring, good rebounding, and low number of fouls.	What is unprofessional behavior? Why is drug use a reason for suspension? What happens when stats are rounded up or down? Can we have statistics for more than 1 year?

Defendable Solution(s)
The three possible solutions are still defendable until more research is done.

This or a similar form is the basic document in the PBL process. It may be structured slightly differently, or it may take two to three pages, but the categories are constant.

Case Name: *Player's Choice, Day 2*

Fact List	Need to Know	Learning Issues

Statistics on players:
 Games played
 Games started
 Minutes played
 Field goals made
 Field goals attempted
 3-point shots made
 3-point shots
   attempted
 Free throws made
 Free throws
   attempted
 Offensive rebounds
 Defensive rebounds
 Assists
 Total rebounds made
 Personal fouls
 Steals
 Turnovers
 Blocks
 Times fouled out
 Total points/season
	What position did the players have when they earned these stats?
	
	 Do they play for an NBA team now? When they earned these stats?
	
	 Did they play in college? Are those stats available?
	
	 How long have they been playing in the NBA?
		Which positions need to be the highest scorers?
		
		 Which positions need to be the best rebounders?
		
		 Which positions need to be best at assists?
		
		 How do coaches make strategies and plays based on the players' statistics?
		
		 Does averaging the statistics for two different years change who the five best players are?

Possible Solutions	New Learning Issues
Any lineup with five players with stats that can be defended. A lineup with five players who have highest field goals, assisting, and high playing time. A lineup with five players who have high scoring, good rebounding, and low number of fouls.	Who will be the coach? What is his record like? How long has he coached? What should a graph include to defend our selected team?

Defendable Solution(s)
Players A, B, D, J, and N

Case Name: *Player's Choice, Day 3*

Fact List	Need to Know	Learning Issues
Centers: A = Kareem Abdul-Jabbar C = Wilt Chamberlain E = Alonzo Mourning *Power forwards:* B = James Worthy F = Dennis Rodman K = Glen Rice *Small forwards:* D = Julius Erving H = Charles Barkley M = Larry Bird *Shooting guards:* J = Michael Jordan L = Pete Maravich O = Clyde Drexler *Point guards:* G = Mugsy Bogues I = John Stockton N = Ervin Johnson	How old is each player on the list? Do any players have old or new injuries that might affect future statistics in any of the areas? Do players get along with each other? Have any been suspended from a team for anything in the past? Have any ever been thrown out of a game?	Compare players' statistics based on number of years played. For example, if stats are for the last 2 years, see if those 2 years are the second and third year played or the sixth and seventh year played. Compare the same years for all players to see if stats change a lot.

Defendable Solution(s)
Players A, B, D, J, and N Defense is provided in graphic presentation prepared for the team owner.

● Appendix E ■

Bibliographic Information for Referenced PBL Problem Resources

This appendix contains annotated descriptions, bibliographic information, and ISBN numbers for books cited as problem case resources in Chapters 2 and 3.

- Bourgeois, P., & Clark, B. (1995). *Franklin wants a pet*. New York: Scholastic. ISBN: 0-590-48915-1. Children are introduced to the concepts of caring for a pet's needs, financially acquiring and keeping a pet, and characteristics of different pets. This story is used with the PBL problem *We'll Take Care of It*.
- Branley, F. M. (1990). *Tornado alert*. New York: Harper Trophy. ISBN: 0064450945.
- Branley, F. M. (1999). *Flash, crash, rumble, and roll*. New York: HarperCollins Juvenile Books. ISBN: 0064451798. These two stories introduce children to the elements of unusual weather and safety issues. They are used as resources for the PBL problem *Weather Watch*.
- Cobb, V. (1981). *Lots of rot*. New York: Scholastic. (Note: This book is now out of print. Suggested replacement is from the Magic School Bus series [1995]. *The magic school bus meets the rot squad*. New York: Scholastic. ISBN: 0-590-40023-1.) This story

introduces children to the concept of decomposition. It is used as a reference with the PBL problem *Where's the Great Pumpkin?*

- Haduch, B. (1999). *Twister!* New York: Dutton Children's Books. ISBN: 0-525-46310-0.
- Harshman, M. (1995). *The storm.* New York: Scholastic. ISBN: 0-590-06861-X.
- Hopping, J. (1995). *Hurricanes!* New York: Scholastic. ISBN: 0-590-46378-0. These three stories introduce children to the elements of unusual weather and safety issues. They are used as resources for the PBL problem *Weather Watch.*
- Ipcar, D. (1976). *Bring in the pumpkins.* (Note: This book is now out of print. Suggested replacement is Kroll, S. [1984]. *The biggest pumpkin ever.* New York: Scholastic. ISBN: 0-590-4643-9. This story introduces children to the concepts of plant growth and cultivation. It is used as a reference with the PBL problem Where's the Great Pumpkin?
- Waters, K. (1993). *Samuel Eaton's day: A day in the life of a Pilgrim boy.* New York: Scholastic Trade. ISBN: 0-590-48053-7.
- Waters, K. (1989). *Sarah Morton's day: A day in the life of a Pilgrim girl.* New York: Scholastic Trade. ISBN: 0-590-44871-4. These two stories are photographic depictions of life in the days of the early settlers. The stories are told from the perspectives of a boy and girl who have lived in this land for 4 years as of 1627.

● References ■

Delisle, R. (1997). *How to use problem-based learning in the classroom.* Alexandria, VA: Association for Supervision and Curriculum Development.

National Research Council. (1996). *The national science education standards.* Washington, DC: National Academy Press.

● Suggested Readings ■

Barrows, H. S. (1988). *The tutorial process.* Springfield: Southern Illinois University School of Medicine.

Dagget, W., & Houston, S. (1998). *Facilitating learning.* New York: Leadership Press.

Delisle, R. (1997). *How to use problem-based learning in the classroom.* Alexandria, VA: Association for Supervision and Curriculum Development.

Gallagher, S., Sher, B., Stepien, W., & Workman, D. (1995). *Implementing problem-based learning in science classrooms.* School Science and Mathematics, 95(3), 136-146.

Schank, R. C., & Cleary, C. (1994). *Engines for education.* Evanston, IL: The Institute for the Learning Sciences.

Stepien, W., & Gallagher, S. (1993). *Problem-based learning: As authentic as it gets.* Educational Leadership, 50(7), 25-28.

Torp, L., & Sage, S. (1998). *Problems as possibilities: Problem-based learning for K-12 education.* Alexandria, VA: Association for Supervision and Curriculum Development.

Van Tassell, G. (2000). *Classroom environment effects on learning.* Retrieved July 18, 2001, from the World Wide Web: http://www.brains.org/environ.htm

● Index ■